G000167686

THE REIGNING KING

KING OF KINGS AND LORD OF LORDS

Lorraine Steele-Deer

THE REIGNING KING. Copyright © 2023. Lorraine Steele-Deer.

All rights reserved. No portion of this book may be reproduced, stored in a retrieval system, or transmitted in any form or by any means—electronic, mechanical, photocopy, recording, scanning, or other—except for brief quotations in critical reviews or articles, without the prior written permission of the author.

www.hcpbookpublishing.com

ISBN-13: 978-1-958404-32-4 (paperback)

Unless otherwise stated, all Scripture quotations are taken from the Amplified® Bible (AMP). Copyright © 2015 by The Lockman Foundation. Used by permission. www.Lockman.org.

DEDICATION

I dedicate this book to the late Queen Elizabeth II.

The Queen's exceptional life of service has left a profound impression on my mind. The accession of her son, King Charles lll, has provided me with a deep revelation of the inheritance we receive in the Kingdom of God through Jesus Christ, the Reigning King.

I strongly believe that despite the upheavals in the royal family, this book presents a ray of hope and a well-timed reminder that Jesus Christ is the "Prince of Peace." Only the King of kings can bring reconciliation, forgiveness, hope, love, mercy, grace, and peace to the monarchy and the rest of the world.

An extract from Queen Elizabeth ll's Christmas message 2011 and 2014 says: *"Forgiveness lies at the heart of the Christian faith. It can heal broken families, it can restore friendships, and it can reconcile divided communities. It is in forgiveness that we feel the power of God's love. For me, the life of Jesus Christ, the Prince of Peace, whose birth we celebrate at Christmas, is an inspiration and an anchor in my life. A role model of reconciliation and forgiveness, He stretched out His hands in love, acceptance, and healing. Christ's example has taught me to seek to respect and value all people of whatever faith or none. Sometimes it seems that reconciliation stands little chance in the face of war and discord. But, as the Christmas truce a century ago reminds us, peace and goodwill have lasting power in the hearts of men and women."*

ACKNOWLEDGMENTS

Above all, I want to offer my sacred honour to God for instructing and guiding me by His Holy Spirit to complete this book within two months.

Special thanks to the supportive family God has blessed me with, my wonderful husband, Steveroy Deer, and our five gorgeous children: Steveroy, Renae, Latavia, Emmanuel, and Gabrielle.

I want to express gratitude to C. Orville McLeish from HCP Book Publishing for publishing the book. Thanks to Osein Olakunle Ibrahim for passionately designing the book cover.

With great reverence, I bow my heart in adoration to Jesus Christ, the Reigning King, who is King and Lord of my life. The treasured moments I spent writing this book have transformed my mind completely and has left the sweet fragrance of Christ lingering in my heart.

But thanks be to God, who always leads us in triumph in Christ, and through us spreads and makes evident everywhere the sweet fragrance of the knowledge of Him. For we are the sweet fragrance of Christ [which ascends] to God, [discernible both] among those who are being saved and among those who are perishing; to the latter one an aroma from death to death [a fatal, offensive odor], but to the other an aroma from life to life [a vital fragrance, living and fresh]. And who is adequate and sufficiently qualified for these things? For we are not like many, [acting like merchants] peddling God's word [shortchanging and adulterating God's message]; but from pure [uncompromised] motives, as [commissioned and sent] from God, we speak [His message] in Christ in the sight of God. (2 Corinthians 2:14-17).

TABLE OF CONTENTS

Precious Mery,

King Jesus delights in
you! You are lovely,
creative and unique

Love & Blessings

INTRODUCTION

The historic moment of Queen Elizabeth II's passing has captured my attention profoundly. The picture reveals a deeper sense of God's sovereign reign over the entire world. The death and resurrection of Jesus Christ is a divine declaration that Jesus is the Reigning King. Our Heavenly Father sent His only Son to be proclaimed King of kings and Lord of lords.

After the death of Queen Elizabeth II, King Charles was officially proclaimed as Britain's new monarch at a palace ceremony where former prime ministers, bishops, and a host of politicians shouted, 'God save the King.' This public statement announces that King Charles III will begin his era of reigning as King of the United Kingdom, the Commonwealth, and the realms.

We are living in a season of sudden changes, and God wants His people to find hope and comfort in knowing that He has sovereign control over the universe.

In the Bible, King David declares:

The Lord reigns, He is clothed with majesty and splendour;
The Lord has clothed and encircled Himself with strength;
the world is firmly established, it cannot be moved. Your
throne is established from of old; You are from everlasting.
(Psalms 93:1-2).

In meditating on this psalm, let us give all glory to "The Reigning King," to whom the heavenly Father has given all power both in heaven and on earth. This declaration sets forth the honour of the kingdom of God and the establishment of His everlasting throne. God upholds and governs the entire world with majesty and indescribable splendour by the kingdom of His grace. The government of God's kingdom over both heaven and earth is put into the hands of Jesus Christ, His only Son. Even before His incarnation, He was Lord of all and the Reigning King over all the realms of creation. We speak of our Reigning King as present because He is worthy to be now seated on the throne as the eternal Word.

We must boldly proclaim the word that Jesus is the Reigning King. Let this resound solemnly before the coronation of another earthly king and throughout all the world:

For to us a Child shall be born, to us a Son shall be given;
And the government shall be upon His shoulder, And His
name shall be called Wonderful Counsellor, Mighty God,
Everlasting Father, Prince of Peace. There shall be no end
to the increase of His government and of peace, [He shall

rule] on the throne of David and over his kingdom, To establish it and to uphold it with justice and righteousness From that time forward and forevermore. The zeal of the Lord of hosts will accomplish this. (Isaiah 9:6-7).

In this book, "The Reigning King," Jesus is celebrated here. The Lord reigns. It is the song of the triumphant church: *Then I heard something like the shout of a vast multitude, and like the boom of many pounding waves, and like the roar of mighty peals of thunder, saying, "Hallelujah! For the Lord our God, the Almighty, [the Omnipotent, the Ruler of all] reigns. (Revelation 19:6).*

Hallelujah; the Lord God omnipotent reigns!

CHAPTER ONE
CLOTHED IN MAJESTY

The LORD reigns, He is clothed with majesty and splendour; The LORD has clothed and encircled Himself with strength; the world is firmly established, it cannot be moved. Your throne is established from of old; You are from everlasting. (Psalms 93:1-2).

Universally, most people know what 'Your Majesty' is all about concerning the Queen's seventy years of reign. It is a title for kings and queens. For example, Queen Elizabeth II was Her Majesty, and King Charles III is now His Majesty. Kings and queens are called "Your Majesty" in recognition of their authority. The English word "majesty" comes from the Latin *maiestas*, which means greatness or dignity. Majesty has to do with splendour; the authority of sovereign power, magnificence, and grandeur. Earthly monarchs have often gone to great lengths to enhance the impression of their Majesty through symbols of power. These symbols represent not only the monarch's reign but also the sovereignty of the nation.

COAT OF ARMS

The function of the royal coat of arms is to identify the person who is Head of State. In the United Kingdom, the royal arms are borne only by the Sovereign. During the Queen's reign, there have been representations of Her Majesty on circulating coinage and banknotes. Another symbol of power is reflected on the miniature head of His or Her Majesty depicted on all stamps and on other significant objects of the royal postal systems. Undoubtedly, the historical crown and jewels of the royal treasures are among the most meaningful symbol of power to be worn by kings and queens.

God doesn't put His image on coins and banknotes, nor stamps or postal objects to show His power. Instead, He allowed His Son, Jesus Christ, to bear His own image and crown Him with glory and honour. On the cross He wore a crown of thorns and thistles, but after His death and resurrection, He was crowned with a symbol of power. The writer of Hebrews captures it well:

But we do see Jesus, who was made lower than the angels for a little while [by taking on the limitations of humanity], crowned with glory and honour because of His suffering of death, so that by the grace of God [extended to sinners] He might experience death for [the sins of] everyone. (Hebrews 2:9).

Jesus Christ became a human being to experience suffering, and the outcome of that suffering of Christ is that He is now crowned with glory and honour. His death provided a divine display of amazing grace. The cross is a universal symbol of the Christian faith and a reminder of Christ's death and the power of His resurrection. The Reigning King Jesus is sovereign over the earthly monarch and does not need to redesign the symbols of His power.

CLOTHED WITH STRENGTH AND SPLENDOUR

God's glory and power are not only displayed through the person of Jesus, but is also in everything He created. In His strength, sovereignty, and greatness, God has created a firmly established world that cannot be moved. God's great strength calls forth honour, and His glory demands worship. In the opening declaration of Psalms 93, King David reminds us that:

The Lord reigns, He is clothed with majesty and splendour; The Lord has clothed and encircled Himself with strength; the world is firmly established, it cannot be moved. Your throne is established from of old; You are from everlasting. (Psalms 93:1-2).

The reality is that Christians sing these words in worship songs, for example, "The Lord Reigns," "Our God Reigns," and "Reign Jesus Reign." Some people put bumper stickers on their cars with this message; many even say these words in prayer and in conversation, yet many believers don't understand how He reigns. God's majesty shines with flashes of fire, and the King of kings is seen in its power in the fall of kingdoms and the collapse of thrones. Being clothed in majesty represents the majestic power and glory from the throne in the heavens above, proclaiming God's sovereign rule.

He is clothed in Majesty and splendour—that is why we worship in spirit and in truth. God's heavenly throne room manifests the glorious and radiant nature of God's kingship.

"He who is the blessed and only Sovereign [the absolute Ruler], the King of those who reign as kings and Lord of those who rule as lords, He alone possesses immortality [absolute exemption from death] and lives in unapproachable light, whom no man has ever seen or can see. To Him be honor and eternal power and dominion! Amen."

God "dwells in unapproachable light." The divine King's glory, His awe-inspiring majesty, His regal radiance is clothed with light.

Being part of the royal family is a great privilege. It comes with the provision of specific types of clothing portraying dignity, traditions, rules, and duty. There is a divine revelation here about God's clothing. God clothed Himself with majesty and glory in the heavens. Clothed in majesty represents the visible lights of the heavens manifesting the greatness and dignity of His sovereign rule as the Reigning King. Psalms 104:1-2 says:

Bless and affectionately praise the Lord, O my soul! O Lord my God, You are very great; You are clothed with splendour and majesty, [You are the One] who covers Yourself with light as with a garment, Who stretches out the heavens like a tent curtain.

God's Majesty is everlasting, and the eternal authority extends to His very being. He is infinite in a sense that none other is; His life is without a beginning and an ending. God stands majestically above His creation. All of creation are ambassadors of God's glory.

As ambassadors of the monarchy, the royal family has a remarkable clothing style. Elegance and modesty dictate the dress code, with members of the family expected to follow certain formalities. Fashion experts and designers help dictate the clothes they wear and how they accessorize them appropriately for different occasions.

Elizabeth II's coronation dress was perhaps the most iconic of her reign. The Queen chose an elaborate gown with the floral emblems of the United Kingdom and her dominions. By working with just a few selected designers throughout her reign, the Queen ensured that her clothes were carefully tailored to the unique demands of her role. Designing for the Queen was no easy task. The Queen tested her clothes thoroughly at fittings. She waved, sat, walked up and down stairs, and modelled outfits with hats and bags. Colour was perhaps the most apparent aspect of her clothing.

THE COLOUR DESIGNER

Be reminded that God is the original designer of colours. The colour blue represents heaven. Blue is the colour of the sky and a reminder of the heavenly realm. Purple represents kingship. In ancient times, purple dye was expensive; therefore, making the colour purple portrays prestige, nobility, kingship, and royalty. This rich colour represents wealth, prosperity, and majesty. Purple reminds us of Jesus because He is the King of kings, and He lives and rules in the hearts of those who are His. It is interesting that the colour purple is made by combining two colours–red, which points to Jesus' blood, His life as a man, and the colour blue, which points to His heavenly dwelling place. Having received forgiveness through His blood, we will one day leave this earth and enter heaven to be with the Reigning King who is clothed in Majesty.

White is the presence of God's unapproachable light. The colour white reminds us of the righteousness of Christ. He wraps Himself in light and righteousness; when a sinner comes to Him in faith, He washes them clean. When Jesus washes us clean from sin, He makes us "white as snow" by giving us His righteousness (see 2 Corinthians 5:21). When Jesus gave Himself for you, He clothed you in righteousness. You are dressed in the finest of white robes! "Who are these, clothed in white robes?" (see Revelation 7:9-17).

Throughout history, clothes serve an essential statutory purpose to reinforce the status of the Monarch and distinguish them from the people surrounding them. The Queen's clothes needed to ensure she looked like a Queen, Her Majesty.

Clothing is essential to human modesty. When it comes to human beings, dress both reveals and conceals. Clothing covers our nakedness, and our clothes communicate something about us. We clothe ourselves in public situations for the sake of dignity, but we unclothe ourselves in privacy.

In our society, typically, you can identify someone by the type of clothes they wear. A businessperson will probably wear a suit; an athlete will wear sporting clothes, and a police officer or soldier will wear a uniform. Sometimes not wearing the right clothes can have drastic consequences, for example, showing up to a wedding in pyjamas.

Garments are used to express authority, status, culture, spiritual well-being, and emotional state. Certain types of clothes in the Bible were worn as an expression of the inner emotional state of the wearer, for example, festive garments, such as for a wedding:

But when the king came in to see the dinner guests, he saw a man there who was not dressed [appropriately] in wedding clothes, and he said, 'Friend, how did you come in here without wearing the wedding clothes [that were provided for you]?' And the man was speechless and without excuse. (Matthew 22:11-12).

The selection of the wedding garment is specific. It would be a sign of disrespect and dishonour to the king to not wear the garment provided for the guests. The man who was caught wearing his old clothing was removed from the celebration. Can you imagine how sorrowful this man was for missing out on the opportunity to enjoy a wedding banquet?

REND YOUR HEART NOT YOUR CLOTHES

The Bible also mentioned sackcloth as a symbol of repentance or sorrow. Those in an extreme state of grief, fear, or anger would tear their clothes (see Genesis 37:29; Isaiah 37:1).

The phrase "rend or rip your heart" expresses internal spiritual brokenness, which is more important than any act of tearing clothing. In this scripture, the prophet Joel expresses this very well:

Rip your heart to pieces [in sorrow and contrition] and not your garments. Now return [in repentance] to the Lord your God, For He is gracious and compassionate, Slow to anger, abounding in lovingkindness [faithful to His covenant with His people]; And He relents [His sentence of] evil [when His people genuinely repent]. Who knows whether He will relent [and revoke your sentence], And leave a blessing behind Him, Even a grain offering and a drink offering [from the bounty He provides you] For the Lord your God? (*Joel 2:13-14*).

Rituals of repentance mean nothing if the heart is not changed because external performances alone can never be sufficient. For this reason, Jesus taught in the Beatitudes, *"Blessed are the poor in spirit, for theirs is the kingdom of heaven." (Matthew 5:3 - KJV).* Being poor in spirit means recognizing one's broken spiritual state. We rend our hearts when we admit that we are utterly broken and destitute before God. Without His forgiveness, cleansing, and restoration, we are undone. Rending our hearts in repentance means wholehearted surrender to God. When we rend our hearts before the Lord, God promises to forgive, cleanse, and restore us. We should all come to the throne of God of grace by faith with sincerity and humility to receive His provision of mercy and forgiveness.

GOD'S PROVISION

God's first response after Adam and Eve sinned was to provide clothing for them as an act of care and mercy (see Genesis 3:21). Clothing symbolizes important provisions for daily life. They can protect, conceal, or display an inner reality of the wearer. A person's level of significance was symbolized by how fancy their clothes were or whether they were provided with the basics of life or with abundant riches. For instance, Isaac gave Joseph a fancy coat to show his importance in the family.

During the Exodus, God showed His preserving power by causing the Israelites' clothes to not wear out. In the armour of God passage in Ephesians 6, we are told to put on the breastplate of righteousness, the belt of truth, and the shoes

21

of peace. Clothing is a sign of victory for conquering kings, so Jesus Himself is clothed with robes of splendour and victory:

"This One (the Messiah) who is majestic in His apparel, Marching in the greatness of His might?"It is I, [the One] who speaks in righteousness [proclaiming vindication], mighty to save." "Who is this, robed in splendour, striding forward in the greatness of his strength?" (Isaiah 63:1).

Yahweh, the Reigning King, is fully clothed, fully encircled in glorious splendour in the greatness of strength. It is a statement of victory! Hallelujah! God is working His plan from His eternal throne. He rules from heaven and has victory over all the kings who rule on the earth.

In society, there is a difference between women's garments and men's garments. Women of the world concern themselves more with their clothes and beauty than perhaps anything else. 1 Peter 3:3-4 says:

"Your adornment must not be merely external—with interweaving and elaborate knotting of the hair, and wearing gold jewelry, or [being superficially preoccupied with] dressing in expensive clothes; but let it be [the inner beauty of] the hidden person of the heart, with the imperishable quality and unfading charm of a gentle and peaceful spirit, [one that is calm and self-controlled, not overanxious, but serene and spiritually mature] which is very precious in the sight of God."

Rather, the godly woman will be clothed with her Christ-like character. Proverbs 31:25 says, *"Strength and dignity are her clothing and her position is strong and secure; And she smiles at the future [knowing that she and her family are prepared]. She is clothed with strength and dignity; she can laugh at the days to come."*

The qualities that this verse describes as the adornment of the godly woman are strength and dignity. These traits fit nicely together as you will not find strength of character without the dignity that accompanies it. True strength of character comes from God clothing us with His strength through the Holy Spirit, and that only comes by spiritual union with God through Christ. She can laugh because she has lived so wisely and is prepared for what may come because she does not think like the women of the world. The godly woman trusts God and relies on the Reigning King.

ATTITUDES AND ACTIONS

Often, in Scripture, clothes identify attitudes or actions inside, instead of focusing on physical garments. God's desire is for us to be joyful and worshipful–to put on a garment of praise. Paul uses the clothing analogy in many passages to describe actions and attitudes a believer must take off or put on. He says in Colossians 3:12:

So, as God's own chosen people, who are holy [set apart, sanctified for His purpose] and well-beloved [by God Himself], put on a heart of compassion, kindness, humility, gentleness, and patience [which has the power to endure

23

whatever injustice or unpleasantness comes, with good temper].

God himself chose us and set us apart. He can exchange our old ways and thoughts for new actions to show the radical transformation that can be created by the Holy Spirit. God exchanges our dirty rags for white linen garments, an external symbol of an internal spiritual change. Putting on and taking off clothes becomes a symbol of a person's spiritual state. The garment of praise is meant to describe how the Lord will minister to our hearts and minds, replacing faulty thoughts with truth and turning every heartbreak into joyful worship. Wearing this new garment allows you to become aligned with His plans and purposes. It leads us to the solemn declaration that Jesus is "the Reigning King" over all our circumstances. Charles Spurgeon writes, "In heaven, none doubt the sovereignty of the King Eternal."

"The LORD is King!" The heavenly robe of majesty that surrounds God when we worship portrays glory and honour. God's heavenly throne room manifests the glorious and radiant nature of God's kingship. Majesty expresses the greatness of appearance and the quality or state of a person or thing that inspires awe or reverence in the beholder.

The majesty and strength of God reveals that He firmly established the world but dwells in eternity. Indeed, it is God who established the world. Not only is the world set, but so is the throne of God forever. His reign is without rivals. There are rulers against His authority, but they will never succeed. Earthly thrones are temporary; they are set up on changeable constitutions, but the throne of Christ is eternal and unchangeable. He was constituted before the foundation of the world.

Even before time began, God reigns as the supreme and omnipotent Monarch, for He is from everlasting to everlasting. There was never a time in which He did not reign over the universe; there can never be an era in which He ceases to reign.

CHAPTER TWO
REIGNING OVER THE REALMS

Nebuchadnezzar the king, to all the peoples, nations, and speakers of every language that live in all the earth: "May your peace abound! It has seemed good to me to declare the signs and wonders which the Most High God has done for me. "How great are His signs and how mighty are His wonders! His kingdom is an everlasting kingdom. And His dominion is from generation to generation. (Daniel 4:1-3).

In a world that seems out of control, it is comforting to know that there is a Reigning King who rules over ALL the realms of heaven and earth. There is a spiritual realm that is a greater reality than the one we are living on earth right now. We see and experience the earthly, but in comparison, the heavenly realm makes the earthly appear to be like a grain of sand in the ocean. Could it be that we are called to focus our full attention on the King who reigns in the heavenly realm rather than the earthly?

THE SPIRITUAL REALM

The spiritual realm is a real world, invisible to the natural eye but visible through the eye of faith. The throne of God is established in heaven, which is in the spiritual realm. God's dwelling is not at a physical location out there somewhere but is now our lives (see 1 Corinthians 6.19). It is all around us, supernaturally, beyond our capacity, strength, imagination, energy, and wisdom. God's realm is a place of total surrender, submission, and dependency on Jesus as the Reigning King. It is when we come to the end of ourselves, rest, rely on, and depend upon Jesus alone. The reign of Jesus will not just take place sometime in the future, it is taking place right now. All that is going on in the heavenly realms is a reality at this very moment. The believer has been raised with Christ and is now seated with Him in the heavenly realms.

"And He raised us up together with Him [when we believed], and seated us with Him in the heavenly places, [because we are] in Christ Jesus." (Ephesians 2:6).

We have a new identity because of our relationship with Christ, and we are granted a new position in heaven. It is because of our heavenly position that Paul calls for us to think on things above (see Colossians. 3:1). We are to be consumed with the things of heaven—God and His kingdom. We are citizens of heaven, consumed with its affairs. Philippians 3:20 says, *"But our citizenship is in heaven. And we eagerly await a Saviour from there, the Lord Jesus Christ."*

There are many examples in history where realms have been ruled by a king. For example, King George V, Edward VIII, and George VI were all kings of the United Kingdom. A monarch holds the highest authority and power in the state. The queen reigned in multiple monarchies simultaneously. For example, the monarchy of Canada and the monarchy of the United Kingdom as well as fourteen other commonwealth realms. Most monarchs, both historically and in the present day, have been born and brought up within a royal family whose rule over a period is referred to as a dynasty.

In a monarchy, a king or queen is the Head of State. The British Monarchy is known as a constitutional monarchy, which means the sovereign is the Head of State. As Head of State, the Monarch undertakes constitutional and representational duties which have developed over one thousand years of the history of Britain.

In addition to these state duties, the Monarch is "Head of Nation." In all these roles, the Sovereign is supported by members of their immediate family. A principal advantage of hereditary monarchy is the immediate continuity of national leadership, as illustrated in the classic phrase "The [old] King is dead. Long live the [new] King!" Traditionally, hereditary succession within members of one family has been the most common mode of electing a king, while an emperor can be elected either by inheritance within the family or by defeating a king.

SOVEREIGN

If you were to look up the word "sovereign" in the dictionary, you would find definitions and phrases like "superior," "greatest," "supreme in power and authority," "ruler," and "independent of all others." But the way I like to explain God's sovereignty best is simply to say, "God is in control." There is absolutely nothing that happens in the universe that is outside of God's influence and authority. As King of kings and Lord of lords, God has no limitations and is omniscient, having universal or complete knowledge. God is in control of all things and rules over all things. He has power and authority over nature, earthly kings, history, angels, and demons. That is what being sovereign means. It means being the ultimate source of all power, authority, and everything that exists. Only God can make those claims; therefore, it is God's sovereignty that makes Him superior to all other gods and makes Him, and Him alone, worthy of worship.

Daniel 4 presents a letter from king Nebuchadnezzar II in which he learns a lesson in relation to God's sovereignty. Nebuchadnezzar dreams of a great tree that shelters the whole world, but an angel appears and decrees that the tree must be cut down, and for seven years he would have his human mind taken away and he would eat grass like an ox. Daniel's role was to interpret the dream for the king. This came to pass, and at the end of his punishment, Nebuchadnezzar bowed His heart in worship to God.

The message of the story is that all earthly power, including that of kings, is subjected to the power of God. *"Let every person be subject to the governing authorities. For there is no authority except from God [granted by His permission and sanction], and those which exist have been put in place by God.' (Romans 13:1).* Nebuchadnezzar learnt that God alone controls the world, and then God restored his earthly kingdom. To the contrary, in Daniel 5, King Belshazzar fails to learn from Nebuchadnezzar's example and has his kingdom taken from him and given to the Medes and Persians.

"The writing on the wall" is often used as a true expression that warns of doom or catastrophe, based on the story of Belshazzar's feast in the book of Daniel. He had not taken the warning through the judgments on Nebuchadnezzar, and he disrespected God. Earthly kings choose to serve and worship gods that neither see, hear or know, but they will be judged by the reigning King who rules over all the realms of creation.

"Then Daniel answered and said before the king, "Keep your gifts for yourself and give your rewards to someone else; however, I will read the writing to the king and reveal the interpretation to him. O king, the Most High God gave Nebuchadnezzar your father a kingdom and greatness and glory and majesty; and because of the greatness that He gave him, all the peoples, nations, and speakers of every language trembled and feared him. Whomever he wished he killed, and whomever he wished he kept alive; whomever he wished he promoted and whomever he wished he humbled.

31

But when his heart was lifted up and his spirit became so proud that he behaved arrogantly, he was deposed from his royal throne and his glory was taken away from him. He was also driven from mankind, and his mind was made like that of an animal, and his dwelling place was with the wild donkeys. He was given grass to eat like cattle, and his body was wet with the dew of heaven until he came to know [without any doubt] that the Most High God rules over the kingdom of mankind and He appoints it to whomever He wills. And you, his son, O Belshazzar, have not humbled your heart (mind), even though you knew all this. And you have exalted yourself against the Lord of heaven, and the vessels of His house have been brought before you, and you and your nobles, your wives and your concubines have been drinking wine from them; and you have praised the gods of silver and gold, of bronze, iron, wood, and stone, which do not see or hear or understand. But the God who holds in His hand your breath of life and your ways you have not honoured and glorified [but have dishonoured and defied]. (Daniel 5:17-23).

Daniel reads the sentence written on the wall:

"Then the hand was sent from the presence [of the Most High God], and this inscription was written: "This is the inscription that was written, 'mene, mene, tekel, upharsin [numbered, numbered, weighed, and divided].' This is the interpretation of the message: 'mene'—God has numbered the days of your kingdom and put an end to it; 'tekel'—you have been weighed on the scales [of righteousness] and found deficient; '[peres'—your kingdom has been divided

and given over to the Medes and Persians. Then Belshazzar gave the command, and Daniel was clothed with purple and a chain of gold was put around his neck, and a proclamation concerning him was issued [declaring] that he now had authority as the third ruler in the kingdom."(Daniel 5:24-29).

Today, all this may well be applied to every earthly kingdom and to every sinner. At death, the sinner's days are numbered and finished; after death is the judgment, when he/she will be weighed in the balance and found wanting; and after judgment, the sinner will be destroyed with the devil and his angels. While these things were passing in the palace, it is considered that the army of Cyrus entered the city, and when Belshazzar was slain, a full submission transpired. On the contrary, Daniel was clothed in purple, wearing gold jewelry, and was given authority and rulership over the kingdom. The writing of God's Word on the wall of our hearts can only be done by the Reigning King, who is indeed the King of kings and the Lord of all lords.

One of the grandest name descriptions of our God is "King of kings and Lord of lords." It is used to declare God's authority over all creation and reminds believers of His power and might. Even Nebuchadnezzar, a very great Old Testament king, came to acknowledge God as His sovereign king in the book of Daniel. God's dominion is an eternal dominion; His kingdom endures from generation to generation.

God's sovereignty calls for our submission. Unlike corrupt earthly kings who abuse their authority to intimidate their subjects, God rules in love. He loves you and wants the best for you. God's sovereignty compels us to bow before Him:

The Lord has established his throne in heaven, and his kingdom rules over all. (Psalm 103:19).

All the peoples of the earth are regarded as nothing. He does as he pleases with the powers of heaven and the peoples of the earth. No one can hold back his hand or say to him: 'What have you done?' (Daniel 4:35).

Some hear this verse and trust that God is in charge, thinking there is no need to worry. Others hear this verse and trust that God is in charge, thinking there is no need to pray. But God specifically invites His people to pray in both the Old Testament and the New. The Apostle Paul encouraged the Christians in Ephesus to pray for kings:

First of all, then, I urge that supplications, prayers, intercessions, and thanksgivings be made for all people, for kings and all who are in high positions, that we may lead a peaceful and quiet life, godly and dignified in every way (I Timothy 2:1-2).

The reality behind our prayers for kings brings great comfort that the Lord reigns over the hearts of earthly kings.

"The king's heart is like channels of water in the hand of the Lord; He turns it whichever way He wishes." (Proverbs 21:1).

34

Since the king's heart is in the Lord's hand, Jesus is truly the King of all kings.

KING OF KINGS

As recently as the early 20th century, the title "King of kings" has been used to describe a great ruler in the Middle East. It applied to a Pharaoh or a monarch who held a higher position than any other kings in a region. But Scripture makes it clear that only our Lord is truly worthy of the title "KING Of KINGS AND LORD OF LORDS."

In the Bible, one of the most remarkable displays of God's sovereign power over an earthly king relates to the story of when God used Moses to speak to Pharoah. This scenario reveals the hardening of the human heart by the sovereign hand of God. Romans 9:17-18 says:

For the scripture says to Pharaoh, 'I raised you up for this very purpose, that I might display my power in you, and that my name might be proclaimed in all the earth.' Therefore, God has mercy on whom He wants to have mercy, and he hardens whom He wants to harden.

So it all comes down to this one mysterious encounter between the sovereign God of the universe and a wicked emperor who sat on a human throne, Pharaoh. The simple command from that Emperor of the universe to that human emperor was *"Let my people go."* There was nothing there too complicated, and Pharaoh knew exactly what God was commanding him to do. What did Pharaoh say? "Who is the

Lord that I should obey Him? I do not know the Lord and I will not let Israel go." (see Exodus 5:2).

God says to Moses, "I will harden Pharaoh's heart." This is a very important statement in Exodus 4:21. God unfolds ten plagues culminating in the dreadful plague on the first born, and then after that, the amazing passage through the Red Sea with Pharaoh's army chasing and then being destroyed in the Red Sea.

"I raised you up." This speaks of God's sovereignty over Pharaoh's position. When God says, "I raised you up for this very purpose," He was saying "I raised you up to be Pharaoh. I raised you up at this time for this purpose. You would not be Pharaoh, if it weren't for My sovereign power." No one can be king over the sovereign power and Lordship of Jesus. This prayer of King David resonates this truth very well:

"Therefore David blessed the Lord in the sight of all the assembly and said, "Blessed (praised, adored, and thanked) are You, O Lord God of Israel (Jacob) our father, forever and ever. Yours, O Lord, is the greatness and the power and the glory and the victory and the majesty, indeed everything that is in the heavens and on the earth; Yours is the dominion and kingdom, O Lord, and You exalt Yourself as head over all. Both riches and honour come from You, and You rule over all. In Your hand is power and might; and it is in Your hands to make great and to give strength to everyone. Now therefore, our God, we thank You, and praise Your glorious name." (1 Chronicles 29:10-13).

CHAPTER THREE
ANOINTED TO SERVE

You prepare a table before me in the presence of my enemies. You have anointed and refreshed my head with - oil; My cup overflows. (Psalms 23:5).

At the Queen's Coronation, the most sacred moment of the ceremony was the anointing. After the symbols of royal status are set aside, wearing a white dress with no jewels or crown, the Queen sat in a sacred moment allowing the archbishop to anoint her with oil. The prayers said over her invited God's Holy Spirit to set her apart as God's royal servant. Many Christians believe that the power is in the oil itself. However, the oil is a symbol of God's approval and dedication to carry out the work of His kingdom here on earth. In the Old Testament, people who were anointed with oil were set apart for special service to God and His people.

OIL

When the Israelites anointed someone, they took olive oil, blended it with expensive spices, then rubbed, smeared, or poured the oil on the head of the person being appointed. In Exodus 30:22-31, special orders were given by God:

Then the Lord said to Moses, "Take the following fine spices: 500 shekels of liquid myrrh, half as much (that is, 250 shekels) of fragrant cinnamon, 250 shekels of fragrant calamus, 500 shekels of cassia—all according to the sanctuary shekel—and a hint of olive oil. Make these into a sacred anointing oil, a fragrant blend, the work of a perfumer. It will be the sacred anointing oil. Then use it to anoint the tent of meeting, the ark of the covenant law, the table and all its articles, the lampstand and its accessories, the altar of incense, the altar of burnt offering and all its utensils, and the basin with its stand. You shall consecrate them so they will be most holy, and whatever touches them will be holy. "Anoint Aaron and his sons and consecrate them so they may serve me as priests. Say to the Israelites, 'This is to be my sacred anointing oil for the generations to come.'"

Priests, prophets, and kings were anointed with this oil. The intended purpose of anointing is to set apart a person, place, or thing for divine use. Anointing kings was a part of the inaugural ceremony of the Jewish Kings (see 1 Samuel 9:16; 10:1; 1 Kings 1:34,39). David was anointed by Samuel in obedience to God's sovereign instructions. So, to be anointed is to be divinely selected and empowered by God to carry out kingdom duties.

In Psalm 23:5, David said to the Lord, *"You prepare a table before me in the presence of my enemies. You have anointed and refreshed my head with oil; My cup overflows."* David had been invited to dine now and forever at the Lord's table and to receive His anointing to serve the people.

In the New Testament, Jesus Christ reveals Himself as our anointed King, Priest, and Prophet. He is God's only begotten Son, the Messiah. In fact, Messiah literally means "anointed one" and is derived from the Hebrew word "Christos," which means Christ "the anointed one." Jesus declared at the launch of His ministry the fulfilment of the prophecy in Isaiah 61:1-3:

The Spirit of the Lord God is upon me, because the Lord has anointed and qualified me to preach the Gospel of good tidings to the meek, the poor, and afflicted; He has sent me to bind up and heal the broken-hearted, to proclaim liberty to the [physical and spiritual] captives and the opening of the prison and of the eyes to those who are bound, To proclaim the acceptable year of the Lord [the year of His favour] and the day of vengeance of our God, to comfort all who mourn, To grant [consolation and joy] to those who mourn in Zion—to give them an ornament (a garland or diadem) of beauty instead of ashes, the oil of joy instead of mourning, the garment [expressive] of praise instead of a heavy, burdened, and failing spirit—that they may be called oaks of righteousness [lofty, strong, and magnificent, distinguished for uprightness, justice, and right standing with God], the planting of the Lord, that He may be glorified.

God anointed His Son, Jesus Christ, to be the Reigning King. When Jesus returned to His hometown synagogue, He opened God's Word and declared that He had been anointed with the Holy Spirit. The Spirit of God Himself anointed Jesus to proclaim the good news of salvation. With His Word, He guides us. With His sacrifice, He redeems us. As our King, He reigns over us and for us.

Perhaps the most important anointing in the Bible happened when a woman from the city approached Jesus while He was having dinner at Simon's house, according to Luke 7:36-38:

One of the Pharisees asked Jesus to eat with him, and He went into the Pharisee's house [in the region of Galilee] and reclined at the table. Now there was a woman in the city who was [known as] a sinner; and when she found out that He was reclining at the table in the Pharisee's house, she brought an alabaster vial of perfume; and standing behind Him at His feet, weeping, she began wetting His feet with her tears, and wiped them with the hair of her head, and [respectfully] kissed His feet [as an act signifying both affection and submission] and anointed them with the perfume.

She anointed Him as the Reigning King, the Messiah. The ultimate purpose of the anointing was to prepare Jesus to fulfil the redemptive plan of God through His death on the cross. Jesus was anointed to do the will of God and He anoints us with His Spirit to serve in His Kingdom. God's anointing fills His people with His love and empowers them to follow Him. What makes this moment so special is that Jesus commended the woman for her faith.

The Queen has acknowledged that her faith in Jesus has been a significant source of strength amidst the vigorous demands and pressures of the role and responsibilities that were bestowed upon her.

Queen Elizabeth II had a strong Christian faith that has been evident throughout her life in her words and actions. Along with her formal role as 'Defender of the Faith and Supreme Governor of the Church of England,' which came with monarchy, her personal faith was evident even before she was crowned. During the Queen's long reign, she was inspired by the sacrificial life of Jesus Christ, who said He "did not come to be served, but to serve."

In 2008, the Queen said: "I hope that, like me, you will be comforted by the example of Jesus of Nazareth who, often in circumstances of great adversity, managed to live an outgoing, unselfish and sacrificial life…He makes it clear that genuine human happiness and satisfaction lie more in giving than receiving; more in serving than in being served. We can surely be grateful that, two thousand years after the birth of Jesus, so many of us are able to draw inspiration from his life and message, and to find in him a source of strength and courage."

In 2016 the Queen said: "Jesus Christ lived obscurely for most of his life, and never travelled far. He was maligned and rejected by many, though he had done no wrong. And yet, billions of people now follow his teaching and find in him the guiding light for their lives. I am one of them because Christ's example helps me see the value of doing small things with great love, whoever does them and whatever they themselves believe."

In 2020 the Queen said, "We continue to be inspired by the kindness of strangers and draw comfort that – even on the darkest nights – there is hope in the new dawn.

Jesus touched on this with the parable of the Good Samaritan. The man who is robbed and left at the roadside is saved by someone who did not share his religion or culture. This wonderful story of kindness is still as relevant today. Good Samaritans have emerged across society showing care and respect for all, regardless of gender, race, or background, reminding us that each one of us is special and equal in the eyes of God.

The teachings of Christ have served as my inner light, as has the sense of purpose we can find in coming together to worship."[1]

---

[1]   https://stjamesandemmanuel.org/extracts-from-the-queens-christmas-message-2000-2021/

ROYAL SERVANTS

Serving the Royal household in any capacity is indeed a privileged opportunity because, whatever the role, all those who help have a great opportunity to serve. They provide invaluable support to the Royal family, enabling them to fulfil their duties and serve the nation. The royal servants work in harmony to ensure the goals of the monarchy are achieved. The Queen, in her duties as Head of State, is served by private secretaries who are responsible for organising official engagements. They also advise on constitutional matters and take responsibility for everything from speeches and correspondence to official presents and congratulatory messages to members of the public.

Many of the teams who serve the royal family have specific assignments to carry out—important official duties such as hospitality, catering, housekeeping arrangements—from garden parties and state visits to royal weddings—and the state opening of parliament as well as the biannual awarding of honours. The Royal Collection Trust is responsible for the care and presentation of the Royal Collection and manages the public opening of the official residences of Her Majesty, the late Queen.

Working members of the royal family will support the King in his many state and national duties, as they did for Her Majesty, Queen Elizabeth, for many years. They also carry out important work in the areas of public and charitable service. Some members of the royal family have also established their own charities such as the Duke of

Edinburgh's Award Scheme and the Princess Royal Trust for Carers, a charity that provides advice and support for people acting as carers.

Serving Jesus is serving royalty. When you serve God, you need to serve Him with great passion and spiritual fervency. When you serve others, you are serving the King of all kings, the Reigning King. As God's child, you are blessed with unique gifts and talents that God uses to help you grow spiritually. Every Christian is called to serve one another and our wider community. Peter wrote in 1 Peter 4:8-10:

Above all, have fervent and unfailing love for one another, because love covers a multitude of sins [it overlooks unkindness and unselfishly seeks the best for others]. Be hospitable to one another without complaint. Just as each one of you has received a special gift [a spiritual talent, an ability graciously given by God], employ it in serving one another as [is appropriate for] good stewards of God's multi-faceted grace [faithfully using the diverse, varied gifts and abilities granted to Christians by God's unmerited favour] As each one has received a gift, minister it to one another, as good stewards of the manifold grace of God.

Christians should strive to fill their time with things that show God is at work in their hearts and lives. Serving one another at church and in the community strengthens your commitment to God, helps you spend time with fellow believers, and gives you a chance to give back to the neighbourhood. As Christians work together and serve others, they also strengthen their faith and witness to the world. As selfless volunteers, they begin to see how each one can make a difference in the world. As you serve the Lord, Jesus, remember Paul's advice in Colossians 3:17, 22-24:

Whatever you do [no matter what it is] in word or deed, do everything in the name of the Lord Jesus [and in dependence on Him], giving thanks to God the Father through Him. Servants, in everything obey those who are your masters on earth, not only with external service, as those who merely please people, but with sincerity of heart because of your fear of the Lord. Whatever you do [whatever your task may be], work from the soul [that is, put in your very best effort], as [something done] for the Lord and not for men, knowing [with all certainty] that it is from the Lord [not from men] that you will receive the inheritance which is your [greatest] reward. It is the Lord Christ whom you [actually] serve.

Just before His death, Jesus decided to give His followers a clear picture of the attitude they should have in serving. He took off his outer garments, got a basin, and washed their feet. The twelve pairs of feet Jesus washed belonged to men who walked rough roads shared with all manner of livestock. Cleaning feet would be the lowly job of a servant. The disciples resisted the idea that their Master and Teacher should stoop to such a humbling task. John 13:12-17 says:

So when He had washed their feet and put on His [outer] robe and reclined at the table again, He said to them, "Do you understand what I have done for you? You call Me Teacher and Lord, and you are right in doing so, for that is

45

who I am. So if I, the Lord and the Teacher, washed your feet, you ought to wash one another's feet as well. For I gave you [this as] an example, so that you should do [in turn] as I did to you. I assure you and most solemnly say to you, a slave is not greater than his master, nor is one who is sent greater than the one who sent him. If you know these things, you are blessed [happy and favoured by God] if you put them into practice [and faithfully do them].

If Jesus humbled Himself in this way—and even further in His death—then we also should be humble in all we do for Him and others. Jesus completed the work of salvation for us on the cross, brings us into it, gives us the Holy Spirit as our counsellor, and sets us about His business. He has finished the work of our salvation, but He still calls us to work for His kingdom. Therefore, with gratitude and love, we train to be the most effective servants possible.

FRIENDS OF THE KING

The Reigning King gives us others to work alongside, a glorious future to work toward, and a promise that our work is not in vain. Most importantly, He gives us Himself, working in us and through us, so that we may be His true friends who are ready and waiting for whenever He comes.

John 15:12-17 says:

This is My commandment, that you love and unselfishly seek the best for one another, just as I have loved you. No one has greater love [nor stronger commitment] than to lay down his own life for his friends. You are my friends if you keep on doing what I command you. I do not call you servants any longer, for the servant does not know what his master is doing; but I have called you [My] friends, because I have revealed to you everything that I have heard from My Father. You have not chosen Me, but I have chosen you and I have appointed and placed and purposefully planted you, so that you would go and bear fruit and keep on bearing, and that your fruit will remain and be lasting, so that whatever you ask of the Father in My name [as My representative] He may give to you. This [is what] I command you: that you love and unselfishly seek the best for one another.

The term "friend" has been used in place of servants. Having knowledge of someone does not mean they are a friend. Being a friend requires a deep relationship, commitment, and loyalty.

But the word "servant" seems to be less appreciated these days. No one really likes to be known as a servant. It seems to portray the idea of being lowly, perhaps even badly treated, and with little or no reward. But when the word is applied to God's people serving God, the word "servant" is royal duty anointed and appointed to us by the Reigning King. The message that stands out in this passage is Jesus saying to His disciples—His servants—that *"I no longer call you servants...but I have called you friends."* Besides being servants, Jesus wanted them to know, and us to know, that His relationship with us exists on a deeper basis than that of being His servants.

CHAPTER FOUR
KINGDOM KEYWORKERS

But seek first his kingdom and his righteousness, and all these things will be given to you as well. (Matthew 6:33).

Akeyworker is someone who does a job that offers essential services to society, for example, a doctor, nurse, teacher or police officer. According to Collins dictionary, "a keyworker is someone without whose work society cannot function properly." Furthermore, an essential worker can be someone who works closely with a particular person and has responsibility for them. Many people consider the title of "essential worker" as a badge of honour. There are many benefits that come from being a keyworker in God's kingdom.

During the COVID-19 pandemic, keyworkers were taking huge personal risks while the rest of us stayed at home in lockdown. They were essential employees who provided a crucial service in supporting and caring for the people who were affected by or dying from the disease. I can recall the weekly round of applause for keyworkers in the UK during this time of global crisis.

Do you consider yourself to be a keyworker in the Kingdom of God? I would recommend that you read the whole chapter of Matthew 10. In the first verse, King Jesus called His twelve keyworkers and gave them instructions for carrying out His essential services:

And Jesus summoned to Him His twelve disciples and gave them power and authority over unclean spirits, to drive them out, and to cure all kinds of disease and all kinds of weakness and infirmity. (Matthew 10:1).

The power and authority that was given was for all the disciples. Their names were stated as recipients of this kingdom mandate. The instructions included a detailed job description concerning the services they were to do; the working of miracles; what they should preach: "The Kingdom of Heaven is at Hand," to whom they must go, how they must behave, and what they can take with them on the mission.

Jesus gave them prophetic knowledge concerning the sufferings they were to endure. They were told that attacks would be from governors and earthly kings. Counsel was given them as to what to do when persecuted, and encouragement was given to bear up cheerfully under their sufferings.

Though these instructions were given directly to the twelve disciples as Kingdom Keyworkers, they are relevant and applicable to all who are essential workers in serving the Kingdom of God today. Throughout the gospel of Matthew, the phrase "kingdom of heaven" is used when referring to the announcement of the rule of Jesus Christ and the good news of His reign.

The Kingdom of Heaven drew near to us when God Himself came to earth as a man. This is what is meant by John when he said, "The Kingdom of heaven is at hand." He implied that the kingdom of heaven is now available today in the person of the reigning King. So, one could say that the kingdom of heaven is a reality now in the present.

"Repent, for the kingdom of heaven is at hand." (Matthew 3:2).

On one occasion, Jesus said, "For indeed, the kingdom of God is within you." (Luke 17:21). He was speaking of Himself. When you are under His kingship, and when He is in control of your life, that is the kingdom of God at work in you as a Kingdom Keyworker. It is not rules and regulations but "righteousness and peace and joy in the Holy Spirit." (Romans 14:17).

Today, Jesus Christ lives and reigns in the hearts of all believers, yet the Kingdom of Heaven will not be completely acknowledged until all evil on the earth is judged and eliminated. Christ first came to earth to live and fulfil the role of a suffering servant. One day, He will return as ruler and judge to govern over all the earth. The individuals who come to Christ as Saviour and recognize Him as the Reigning King are granted citizenship into the heavenly realm, the kingdom of the Son. They have a place with Jesus now. Christians have a closer connection with Jesus than those of a royal family or an earthly king.

Jesus told Pilate when he was put on trial:

"My kingdom is not of this world [nor does it have its origin in this world]. If My kingdom were of this world, My servants would be fighting [hard] to keep Me from being handed over to the Jews; but as it is, My kingdom is not of this world." So Pilate said to Him, "Then You are a King?" Jesus answered, "You say [correctly] that I am a King. This is why I was born, and for this I have come into the world, to testify to the truth. Everyone who is of the truth [who is a friend of the truth and belongs to the truth] hears and listens carefully to My voice." (John 18:36-37).

KINGDOM KEYS

Keys are used to lock or unlock doors. As keyworkers, we are given the authority of locking and unlocking or opening and closing doors both spiritually and practically. One of the most common purposes of keys is that they give us security and protection. We can lock our doors and know that no one else has the key. We have keys to our homes, to our belongings, to suitcases, to cars, and we carry keys when we are away from home. When you get a job, depending on your role, you are given keys to gain access to the building or office. Locks and keys affect our lives in various ways. Sometimes a key means the difference between freedom and captivity or life and death.

In Matthew 16:19, we read of the Lord Jesus saying to Peter:

And I will give to you the keys of the kingdom of heaven: and whatever you shall bind on earth shall be bound in heaven: and whatever you shall loose on earth shall be loosed in heaven.

The specific keys Jesus had in mind open the doors to release people from captivity here on earth so they can be free to enter His Heavenly Kingdom. In ancient times, keys were symbols of authority. The grave and Hades were considered places where people were bound and held captive. Jesus wanted His followers to know that He alone had the power and authority to free them from the shackles of death and give them eternal life:

But God, being [so very] rich in mercy, because of His great and wonderful love with which He loved us, even when we were [spiritually] dead and separated from Him because of our sins, He made us [spiritually] alive together with Christ (for by His grace—His undeserved favour and mercy—you have been saved from God's judgment). And He raised us up together with Him [when we believed], and seated us with Him in the heavenly places, [because we are] in Christ Jesus. (Ephesians 2:4-6).

Not even the grave could hold the Reigning King. Though He died on the cross and was buried in a tomb, the Messiah rose from the dead and now lives forevermore. His victory through the resurrection enabled Him to control the keys of death and Hades. All human authorities were mortal and limited, whereas the Reigning King is immortal and infinite in power. This means His essential nature is characterized by life.

Under the Reigning King, the disciples were keyworkers of the Kingdom of Heaven. Keyworkers hold keys—that is you and me. We hold keys to open and close doors in the spiritual through our prayers and declarations.

Jesus opens the door to heaven and invites the world to enter in. Jesus said:

I am the door. If anyone enters by Me, he will be saved, and will go in and out and find pasture. The thief does not come except to steal, and to kill, and to destroy. I have come that they may have life, and that they may have it more abundantly. (John 10:9-10).

In this "I am" statement, Jesus points out for us the exclusive nature of salvation by saying that He is "the door," not "a door." Jesus is the only means we have of receiving eternal life (see John 3:16). There is no other way. It is awesome that Jesus is the only door and gives keyworkers the keys to His Kingdom. The benefits of being a kingdom keyworker are found in the Word of God. God promises us that we will be with Him even to the end of this age.

Working for the kingdom of heaven is much more rewarding than any earthly job. In fact, our earthly jobs should be yet another opportunity for kingdom building. Regardless of our occupations or titles, we must get our news and take our instructions from the living Word and not the world. What is popular and acceptable in the world will continue to change. There will always be uncertainties, sudden changes, and growing instability, but Jesus remains the same yesterday, today, and forevermore (see Hebrews 13:8).

In His sermon on the mount, recorded in Matthew 6:33, Jesus said:

First and most importantly seek (aim at, strive after) His kingdom and His righteousness [His way of doing and being right—the attitude and character of God], and all these things will be given to you also.

We are to seek the things of God as a priority over the things of the world.

Then Jesus said to his disciples, 'Whoever wants to be my disciple must deny themselves and take up their cross and follow me.' (Matthew 16:24).

As a kingdom keyworker, you align with God's lordship by believing what God has said in His Word. When you choose to make Him Lord and King, you give Him the right to have the final authority over every decision and choice you make in your life. Jesus is the Reigning King, and we must live under His kingdom authority—a kingdom that is ruled and controlled by God. The authority to rule was given to Jesus Christ by the Father, and Jesus is now situated at the right hand of the Father in heaven.

THY KINGDOM COME

In what is commonly referred to as the "Lord's Prayer," we are taught to pray not only for God's will to take control of our lives, but for His kingdom to come throughout the earth. We have become a part of God's kingdom when we repent of all our sins and accept the sacrifice of Jesus Christ. We are then called to be keyworkers, to tell others about Him, and that we would remain surrendered to His will for our lives. Jesus taught us to pray:

This, then, is how you should pray: "Our Father in heaven, hallowed be your name, your kingdom come, your will be done, on earth as it is in heaven. Give us today our daily bread. And forgive us our debts, as we also have forgiven our debtors. And lead us not into temptation, but deliver us from the evil one." (Matthew 6:9-13a).

"Your kingdom come. Your will be done on earth as it is in heaven." This is praying for a day when God will bring heaven to earth and bring His rule on this world. God still has a plan for Jesus to rule and reign over all the nations and governments of the world, and as believers, we will rule and reign with Him. Christ will return, then carry this rule from heaven to earth. Christ will reign with the authority and power of earth and of heaven.

God has equipped the church as His keyworkers worldwide to teach the gospel (good news) of the Reigning King Jesus. As Christians, our identity is shaped by the teachings and character of Jesus. Therefore, in the kingdom God, the attitudes and traits of Christians should be the same. From the personality of the believer comes his/her thoughts, actions, and deeds. Only the spiritual man can live under the governance of the kingdom of God. There is greater work to be done in preparation for His return when He comes as the Reigning King of all kings. He told His disciples that only the Father knew when the time would be right. Until then, His people are to be involved in a special work right up until the end of the age:

And He said to them, 'It is not for you to know times or seasons which the Father has put in His own authority. But you shall receive power when the Holy Spirit has come upon you; and you shall be witnesses to Me in Jerusalem, and in all Judea and Samaria, and to the end of the earth.' (Acts 1:7-8).

CHAPTER FIVE
BORN TO BE KING

King Charles III, formerly known as the Prince of Wales, was born in 1948, and became heir on the ascension of Queen Elizabeth II to the throne in 1952 when he was just three years of age. At age four, Charles was famously shown seated between the Queen Mother and Princess Margaret at Elizabeth's coronation ceremony, and continued to spend his life in the public eye.

On September 8, 2022, following the death of his mother, King Charles III ascended to the throne at age seventy-three. Britain's longest-serving heir-apparent was officially proclaimed king two days later at a ceremony at St. James's Palace near Buckingham Palace, making him the oldest person to assume the title.

The author, Catherine Mayer, wrote a book titled "Born to be King" about Prince Charles. Published in 2015, "Born to Be King" explains how and why Charles may redefine the role of the sovereign, even as it reveals the astonishing extent to which the prince has already left his mark on the world. The preface to the book says:

Prince Charles has spent his entire life preparing to be king while insisting on being his own man. In this brilliant portrait, he emerges as a complex character driven by a painful past, a questing intellect, and a powerful impulse not only to reshape the monarchy but to use the long wait for the throne to work toward high ideals. But in aiming to be a King, he often creates heartache for himself and others.

Until more recent times, all royal babies were born in Buckingham Palace. Prince Charles was born at Buckingham Palace on the evening of November 14, 1948, and Princess Elizabeth was just twenty-two years old at the time. You could say this was the nativity of King Charles III. Nativity is a fancy way of saying "birth." If a new mother says, "My baby's nativity was gorgeous!" people might not know what she means. But the word "nativity" is mostly used specifically about the birth of Jesus Christ. This can be in the form of a play usually performed by children at Christmas that tells the story of the birth of Jesus in a manger in Bethlehem.

THE NEWBORN KING

One of the most remarkable moments in history was when the virgin Mary gave birth to Jesus, her firstborn Son. Announcing the birth of Jesus, the angel Gabriel brought an important message to Mary:

And behold, you will conceive in your womb and bring forth a Son and shall call His name JESUS. He will be great and will be called the Son of the Highest; and the Lord God will give Him the throne of His father David. And He will reign over the house of Jacob forever, and of His kingdom there will be no end. (Luke 1:31-33).

Jesus was born in Bethlehem when Herod was king of Judea. Some men who studied the stars came from the east to Jerusalem and asked, "Where is the Baby born to be the king of the Jews?" They had seen his star in the east and come to worship him. The truth is that "Jesus was born King" not just of the Jews but "King of kings" and they came to worship Him because even as a baby, He alone is worthy of worship. He is the King sent from heaven and into the manger where Mary and Joseph stayed to behold their baby boy. He carried the divine title of 'The Reigning King.'

Herod was upset and called the chief priests and teachers of the law and asked them "Where will the Messiah be born?" They told him Bethlehem had been predicted in prophecy. Herod asked the visitors to let him know exactly where the child was, so he too could worship Him. They followed the star until it stopped over the place where the child laid. They worshipped Him and brought out their gifts of gold, frankincense, and myrrh. They returned home by another road as God had warned them in a dream not to return to Herod.

Herod faced a threat to his rule and was keen to locate the baby. The Old Testament prophecies of the prophet Micah had written about Bethlehem, "Out of you will come a ruler who will be the shepherd of my people Israel." (see Micah 5:2). The conclusion therefore was that *the new* King would be born in Bethlehem.

During the Christmas season, we have heard that Jesus Christ was born in a manger among animals, but how many people really accept that He was born as the Reigning King? From His very birth, Christ was recognized as King. Shepherds bowed down and worshiped Him, and angels, knowing more than men, knew that He was truly King. Even the manger acknowledged His sovereign throne.

Jesus was born in Bethlehem, while Herod was born in Edom. Jesus, the Messiah, was sinless; Herod, the king of the Jews, was full of sin and cruelty. Herod had only earthly power and stored no treasures in the kingdom of heaven. Jesus had no need to seek worldly power because He was given power both in heaven and on earth. Matthew 28:18 says:

Jesus came up and said to them, "All authority (all power of absolute rule) in heaven and on earth has been given to Me."

God allowed these two kings, the Reigning King Jesus and King Herod, to present a contrast in the same moment of history. What was he trying to reveal about Himself through this contrast? Jesus gave His life and ministry as a sacrifice so that the world would know God, but Herod's life revolved around sacrificing others to bring glory and honour to himself. Jesus and Herod were opposites in every way; morally, culturally, spiritually, and especially in terms of their worldly status. The contrast of Herod and Jesus reminds Christians to follow God's ways rather than the world's ways. Ultimately, we create a legacy through self-sacrifice and servanthood, not through self-glorification. Jesus, the Reigning King, sought first to do the will of His Father in heaven; to please, honour, and glorify Him. Jesus also came to bring people abundant life, which required Him to lose His life and then be resurrected to return to heaven.

WHY WAS JESUS BORN?

God created Adam and Eve and placed them in a beautiful environment that supplied their every need. In the Garden of Eden, our original human parents found food plentiful, friendly animals, and a loving Father and faithful Friend. God Himself shared divine fellowship with the couple, and they experienced perfect peace, a holy community and supernatural joy. If Adam and Eve had obeyed God, they would have had access to the tree of life instead of the tree of evil and death. Eve was deceived by the serpent, so she ate the forbidden fruit and presented the same fruit to her husband. Adam also ate the fruit of the tree of the knowledge of good and evil.

God's great plan for mankind included the need for a Saviour and Redeemer of mankind. Jesus Christ was born and lived on earth for a little more than three decades. God planned for Christ to be born a King. He knew only His Son could overcome the darkness of the evil king of this world, Satan, the devil.

Jesus Christ was born to reign over the nations of the earth, and He clearly understood there is no end to His Kingdom.

And, behold, thou shalt conceive in thy womb, and bring forth a son, and shalt call his name Jesus. He shall be great, and shall be called the Son of the Highest: and the Lord God shall give unto him the throne of his father David: And he shall reign over the house of Jacob for ever; and of his kingdom there shall be no end. (Luke 1:31-33 - KJV).

All over the world, the Christmas message is dramatized and retold by millions of children. Although we may know the story of Mary and Joseph giving birth to a baby in a manger, we don't truly grasp the importance, in today's world, of the birth of Jesus Christ, God's only Son—the greatest gift that God has ever given. We have taken that for granted.

The Saviour had to be born because mankind, after the sin of Adam and Eve, would have been eternally lost—separated from God forever. That is why Jesus came to earth and allowed Himself to be sacrificed to save mankind. Jesus had to be born because God wanted to reveal His own character to humanity. Jesus is the mediator of the New Covenant. Under the New Covenant, God replaced the sacrifices of the Levitical priesthood with the ultimate sacrifice of Jesus Himself.

But as it is, Christ has acquired a [priestly] ministry which is more excellent [than the old Levitical priestly ministry], for He is the Mediator (Arbiter) of a better covenant [uniting God and man], which has been enacted and rests on better promises. (Hebrews 8:6).

The heavenly Father's divine love and sovereign justice needed a mediator as a "go between"—between God and man—to execute love and justice with one acceptable sacrifice. Through Christ, God has restored that which was lost in Eden, giving us free access to the tree of life. God has made it possible for all people to enter an intimate relationship with Him—which is why Jesus had to be born. God has made it possible for all mankind and whosoever is willing to come into an intimate relationship with Him. This could not have been possible, in God's great plan, without the birth and subsequent sacrifice of His Son, Jesus Christ.

His disciples wondered when Jesus would take over as King. They asked the risen Christ, "Lord, will You at this time restore the kingdom to Israel?" (Acts 1:6b). In the minds of the apostles, the messianic King would soon bring freedom from Roman oppression and usher in the peace and prosperity pictured by prophecies they had heard since childhood. According to Matthew 1, Jesus Christ is a direct descendant of David. As Messiah (the anointed One), He will inherit David's throne, and He will also become the King of kings over the whole world.

BORN FROM ABOVE

Every child is born into a family, and there is a desire within everyone to be a part of a loving family. In a world of broken marriages/relationships and dysfunctional families, that need becomes greater. We had no choice of our earthly family, but we do have a choice to enter God's family through faith in the Reigning King, the Son of God. Jesus calls this spiritual birth being "born again."

As Jesus talked with Nicodemus, He said, 'I tell you the truth, no one can see the kingdom of God unless he is born again.' 'How can a man be born when he is old?' Nicodemus asked. 'Surely he cannot enter a second time into his mother's womb to be born!' Jesus answered, 'I tell you the truth, no one can enter the kingdom of God unless he is born of water and the Spirit. Flesh gives birth to flesh, but the Spirit gives birth to spirit. You should not be surprised at my saying, "You must be born again"' (John 3:3-7). The phrase "born again" literally means "born from above."

Nicodemus had a real need. He needed a change of his heart—a spiritual transformation. New birth, being born again, is an act of God whereby eternal life is imparted to the person who believes in the death of His Son on the cross. Being "born again" also carries the idea of "becoming children of God" through trust in Jesus Christ, the Reigning King.

The question naturally comes, "Why does a person need to be born again?"

Every individual who is born-again has repented of their sins and turned to Christ for their salvation, and as a result, has become a part of God's family forever. All this takes place as God's Holy Spirit works in our lives because of the death and resurrection of His Son as Saviour and Reigning King. Jesus Christ came to save us and to make us part of His family forever. He did this by dying for our sins on the cross and by conquering death through His resurrection.

As a son or daughter, you were born into an earthly family. But when we come to Christ, we are spiritually reborn into another family—the family of God, and nothing can change that.

Since by your obedience to the truth you have purified yourselves for a sincere love of the believers, [see that you] love one another from the heart [always unselfishly seeking the best for one another], for you have been born again [that is, reborn from above—spiritually transformed, renewed, and set apart for His purpose] not of seed which is perishable but [from that which is] imperishable and immortal, that is, through the living and everlasting word of God. (1 Peter 1:22-23).

God both knew and crafted your destiny before you were born. King David said:

Yet you brought me out of the womb; you made me trust in you, even at my mother's breast. From birth I was cast on you; from my mother's womb you have been my God. (Psalm 22:9).

67

Psalm 71:6 says:

From birth I have relied on him; he brought me forth from my mother's womb. I will ever praise him, my God and Heavenly Father.

The fact that God knit you together in your mother's womb means you are fearfully and wonderfully made. In Psalms 139:13 we read, "He created my inmost being; he knit me together in my mother's womb." You have been created in God's image, and you are unique. There is no one else quite like you. He knits the child together with a specific genetic DNA (Divine Nature and Attributes). He lovingly and skilfully weaves together the various parts to make a beautiful person. That is a message a lot of us need to hear today because a lot of people don't really like themselves. They wish God had made them differently. Be assured that God made you just the way He wanted you to be. You are the work of a master craftsman who personally fashioned you in the womb as a unique and beautiful work of God.

Every child born into the world is completely helpless, dependent, and desperately in need of care and protection. So it is with every child who is born into the kingdom of God. Kingdom entrance first depends on our coming to God in total helpless dependence. We often think a child cannot come to God until he is an adult, but an adult cannot receive the Kingdom of God until he/she becomes helpless and dependent like a child.

Jesus' words are true, *"Truly, truly, I say to you, unless one is born again, he cannot see the kingdom of God."* (John 3:3, and *"Truly, I say to you, unless you turn and become like children, you will never enter the kingdom of heaven."* (Matthew 18:3).

A little child takes food, love and protection from their parents' or carers as a gift without beginning to think of whether as a child it is deserved or they do well enough to merit such attention. So must we all receive God's kingdom and enter it with childlike faith.

CHAPTER SIX
THE ROYAL PICTURE FRAME

For this reason [grasping the greatness of this plan by which Jews and Gentiles are joined together in Christ] I bow my knees [in reverence] before the Father [of our Lord Jesus Christ], from whom every family in heaven and on earth derives its name [God—the first and ultimate Father]. (Ephesians 3:14-15).

Photographs play an important role in everyone's life. They connect us to our past; they remind us of people, places, feelings, and stories. They can help us to know who we are. Images are the collection of external messages that we communicate about our inner selves. We communicate these messages not just through our appearance but through our actions, speech, and lifestyles. Everything we say and do communicates something about us. They say a "picture paints a thousand words," meaning having good photos and images can truly enhance our understanding and reveal a bigger picture.

ROYAL PHOTOS

Recently, there has been an increase in the public posting of royal photographs, especially when it comes to pictures of the younger generation. We can observe a decline in the employment of professional photographers by the royal palaces. While a professional photographer used to be invited to take photographs for every royal occasion, today, this has often been limited to official portraits, family pictures, christenings, anniversaries, and weddings. Of course, photographs taken by members of the royal families have always existed, but it was rather rare that these images were officially shared by the royal courts.

The shift in official photographs means that pictures taken of the Royal Family gives a personal touch. The young princes and princesses will often be more at ease because the photo is taken by their parents or family members. A professional photographer does not have to be welcomed in the private environment, which is less invasive, for example, when the first baby pictures are taken. Social media has become the perfect informal platform to share pictures taken by the members of the royal family themselves.

Since the death of Queen Elizabeth II, Buckingham Palace has unveiled a new official photo of the King and Queen Consort with the Prince and Princess of Wales. The elegant photograph is the first official image of King Charles III with the new heir. Released by Royal Communications on the evening of Saturday, October 1, 2022, the accompanying announcement reads: 'A New Image of Their Majesties The King.'

The Palace also released a new official photograph of the King, unveiled on Friday, September 23, 2022. Taken in the Eighteenth Century Room at Buckingham Palace, the image showed His Majesty carrying out duties from the monarch's Red Box–continuing a tradition favoured by his mother, who was photographed with her famous despatch box on many occasions throughout her reign.

When God wants to teach us certain truths, He essentially says, "Picture a father and a son, or picture a wife and a husband, or picture a brother and sister or picture a child or picture a mother and her nursing baby." Because He made these family relationships to be universal, He can use them as pictures in every context and in every age. So, if we understand family, we have a godly framework that helps us understand certain truths about God. If we overlook the significance of family or reframe God's original family picture, we will not grasp the full understanding of who God really is. The family comes from God, the Father, and was established in heaven before being on the earth. The Apostle Paul wrote:

For this reason [grasping the greatness of this plan by which Jews and Gentiles are joined together in Christ] I bow my knees [in reverence] before the Father [of our Lord Jesus Christ], from whom every family in heaven and on earth derives its name [God—the first and ultimate Father]. (Ephesians. 3:14-15).

73

Every family in heaven and on earth is called a family because God gives it that name. It is amazing that all around the world, in every country and every society, the family unit exists. It is usually a husband and wife and a number of children. The family is one of God's great gifts to humanity. It carries the essence of friendship, strength, service, love, and care. On the last day of creation, God, our heavenly Father, finished His picture of creation with a personal touch. Genesis 1:26-27 says:

Then God said, "Let Us (Father, Son, Holy Spirit) make man in Our image, according to Our likeness [not physical, but a spiritual personality and moral likeness]; and let them have complete authority over the fish of the sea, the birds of the air, the cattle, and over the entire earth, and over everything that creeps and crawls on the earth." So, God created man in His own image, in the image and likeness of God He created him; male and female He created them.

You are a picture of God's magnificent artwork. A piece of art is an expression of the artist. It brings glory and honour to the creator. God made you as a reflection of His glory. God created you in His image. After making all the animals in the world, the heart of God was still not satisfied. He desired to create something unique, something special, something that would reflect His image.

LIKE FATHER, LIKE SON

It is impossible to see God since He is a spiritual being. Hence, nobody will be able to show you an actual photograph of God. What we can see, however, is an exact image of God through His Son, Jesus. Every time Jesus spoke about God, He called Him Father. He is your Father, our heavenly Father, a real loving and caring Father. We see His love, power, goodness, grace, and the way He comforts us is very real. Jesus Christ revealed God perfectly.

He is the exact living image [the essential manifestation] of the unseen God [the visible representation of the invisible], the firstborn [the preeminent one, the sovereign, and the originator] of all creation. For by Him all things were created in heaven and on earth, [things] visible and invisible, whether thrones or dominions or rulers or authorities; all things were created and exist through Him [that is, by His activity] and for Him. And He Himself existed and is before all things, and in Him all things hold together. [His is the controlling, cohesive force of the universe.] He is also the head [the life-source and leader] of the body, the church; and He is the beginning, the firstborn from the dead, so that He Himself will occupy the first place [He will stand supreme and be preeminent] in everything. For it pleased the Father for all the fullness [of deity—the sum total of His essence, all His perfection, powers, and attributes] to dwell [permanently] in Him (the Son), and through [the intervention of] the Son to reconcile all things to Himself, making peace [with believers] through the blood of His cross; through Him, [I say,] whether things on earth or things in heaven. (Colossians 1:15-20).

This ancient proverb, "like father, like son" is a true expression of God, the Father, and Jesus, His only begotten

Son. When a son shows similarities to his father in mannerisms, interests, and behaviour, this phrase is aptly used. It can sometimes be used in reference to physical likeness as well.

As mentioned in the gospel of John, Phillip was not persuaded that Jesus bears the exact image of the Father, so he said "Lord, show us the Father, and we will be satisfied." Jesus' response was "Have I been with you all this time, Phillip, and you still do not know me? Whoever has seen me has seen the Father." (see John 14:7-10). Jesus echoes the phrase "like father, like son." No one has ever seen God. It is God, the only Son, who is close to the Father's heart, literally, from the heart or bosom of the Father.

This is the whole of Jesus' mission, to make known the Father, to reveal who God is. Jesus came from the bosom of the Father and is now ascended to heaven as the Reigning King. If we want to know who God is, we need look no further than Jesus. All the words that Jesus has spoken, all the works that He has done, come from God and show us who God is. "He who has seen me has seen the Father," taken literally, seems to suggest that the Father looks exactly like the Lord Jesus Christ. This is the fullest revelation of the person and character of God.

The Word of God, inspired by the Holy Spirit, gives us a clear picture of the sovereign relationship between the Father and His Son, Jesus, to help us understand who God is. Scriptures describing photos of God show you how beautiful God is and the depth of His sovereignty, perfection, and plan of redemption.

This universal idea of the kingdom of God is one of divine family. So, the church represents God's kingdom, and we are all sons and daughters of God. *"And I will be a Father to you, and you will be My sons and daughters," Says the Lord Almighty." (2 Corinthians 6:18).* Christ, the Reigning King, reconciled us to God and united us as a family. He joins us in communion with all those who have already been accepted in the kingdom of God.

CHOOSING THE RIGHT FRAME

Picture frames provide protection. Whether your pictures are personalised prints, family photos or magnificent oil paintings worth millions, they all benefit from protection. A frame protects the edge of the picture as well as the front and back. A frame helps your picture to remain valuable whether it is of sentimental value or monetary value.

Picture frames separate the picture contained within from the room outside. A frame acts as a visual barrier so that when you are looking at a picture, you know immediately where the edge is, and you are not distracted by whatever surrounds it. The thicker the frame, the stronger the barrier. A frame helps you focus and concentrate on the picture, and in this sense, a frame lets you know what the artist wanted you to see—it is a boundary between what is important (the art) and everything else.

Picture frames, like all home decor, says something about the person who chose them. Whatever your choice of picture frames, as well as the pictures they display, shows your personal style. Frames, like wall art, make a statement. The frame not only separates the picture from the space it is in; it also joins it to that space, so picture frames are an important part of the interior decor of a room. Picture frames separate the picture contained within one room from other rooms. A frame helps you focus and concentrate on the picture because the attention is drawn to the painting rather than its frame.

The history of picture frames in the Royal Collection is one of changing tastes and styles. Over the centuries, many monarchs have had their paintings reframed to reflect the fashion of the day. King Charles III, at his new office, placed a new framed photo on the table. It shows Charles alongside his mother, the Queen, his son, William, and grandson, Prince George. The photo reflects "the start of a new decade."

While not all frames may be masterpieces of craftsmanship, they exist in space with their pictures and so should ideally complement them; an elaborate frame will not always suit a simple picture and, by the same token, a large, grand portrait may lack grandeur in a small, plain frame. In most cases, our images of a frame are presented to allow the object to be appreciated for its own merits.

God expresses His message of glory and majesty through imagery in the Bible. Each image deepens the impact of

God's Word on our hearts and mind. They reach deep into our souls to call out our experiences of the past so that we can better appreciate the message being conveyed.

FAMILIES

We are part of the family of All Creation. We care for the things God has made, and we also notice how God cares for us through these same things. We are challenged to delight in the natural world and consider our responsibility to nurture and protect it.

Our family here on earth is like a picture frame of the family in heaven. In the same way we can go to our parents for advice, our heavenly Father is always there to give us help. When we pray, He listens, and He answers. This family is a heavenly picture, which is more real than an earthly one. God loves us so much. He loves us even when we make mistakes, and He always invites us with open arms to return to Him. We glimpse our heavenly Father's perfect love for us in the profound love many parents have for their children. We can all experience our heavenly Father's love as we grow closer to Him, and we can share that love with our families.

Families are central to God's plan for His children. They are the fundamental building block of strong societies. Families are where we can feel love and learn how to love others. Life is tough, and we need people we can lean on. Home should be a safe place where we can get love, advice, and support.

Remember, God sees the bigger picture. He sees the beginning and the end. The Bible gives us vivid images, from visions, to detailed explanations and accounts of places and events, to symbolic imagery used to explain parables. They are used to teach and encourage the first-century churches, and are driving forces within the Biblical text. Metaphorical language, as well as the literal meaning of the characteristics of God, tell the story. Through the divine help of the Holy Spirit, we can communicate profound truths about the reality of the frame of mind in which we understand God. First, family pictures the Trinity. If you don't understand family, you cannot understand God Himself. Why? Because God reveals the first person of the Trinity as God, the Father, and the second person of the Trinity as God, the Son. Of course, this Father-Son relationship is not identical to our father-son relationships, but it does help us understand that they relate and interact as Father and Son. Imagine there was a royal family with no fathers and sons.

For God [the Father] so loved the world that he gave his only Son that whoever believes in him should not perish but have eternal life. (John 3:16).

If you don't understand the powerful, natural love and protection of a Father for His Son, how could you understand what it costs God to provide His beloved Son as a sacrifice?

This is one reason fatherlessness is harmful—it removes the point of comparison between our fathers on earth and our much greater Father in heaven. Fathers who abuse their children are committing a terrible offence—they are giving a false picture of the way God, the Father, relates to us, His children. Therefore, we need to be concerned about same-sex relationships—in a partnership where there are only two mothers, the sovereign picture of God as Father is wrongly framed. God has given us family as a way to picture other things, a way to understand other realities. The more our families look like God's design for families, the clearer those pictures will become, and the closer people will be to understanding. Your family portraits bring your family together. It reminds your family of its love for one another. Your family portraits bring joy, and in hard times, your family portraits can bring comfort and can heal.

Here is another reason family portraits are so important. Did you know the simple act of having your families' photographs hung in your house increases your children's self-esteem? Studies show that having your family photographed and your loving portraits displayed prominently in your home sends the message that your family is important to one another, and that you honour the memories you created together.

Throughout the New Testament, the body of Christ, the church, the bride of Christ, and the Kingdom of God are most commonly used to frame our minds to think like Christ: having the mind of Christ as the Reigning King. Paul utilized imagery because it was something with which his audiences were already familiar; however, he places a different spin on the deeper meaning of a united body. First Corinthians explains the body of Christ to be one body with many members, each of value and contributing to the overall success and function of the body. The body of Christ is to create a unity of believers; many different people with different gifts all striving toward one goal in Christ. Paul explained that the body of Christ is formed from all believers, baptized in Christ, and that baptism is of one spirit and therefore of one body. Additionally, believers are all given different gifts and different abilities from those gifts; however, the point of the gifts is the glory of Christ. All gifts come from one God, and should, in turn, be utilized to bring believers closer to Him. A single gift on its own is not as powerful as many gifts combined; therefore, the body of Christ needs unity to allow all things to work together for the best results and ultimate glory to God. The body should be recognized as one whole with many contributing parts affirming that within the body there is not only unity, but diversity.

From Him the whole body [the church, in all its various parts], joined and knitted firmly together by what every joint supplies, when each part is working properly, causes the body to grow and mature, building itself up in [unselfish] love. (Ephesians 4:16).

Paul is urging the members of the church in Ephesus to be a unified group despite cultural differences that could come between them. Unity, as presented in Ephesians 4, is not attainable by man's desires alone but rather a gift from the Spirit. This gift is offered to any believer "baptized in the name of Christ;" however, it is necessary that believers work to cultivate and nurture the gift of unity to serve the Reigning King.

CHAPTER SEVEN
HEIRS TO THE THRONE

He will call out to me, 'You are my Father, my God, the Rock my Saviour.' And I will appoint him to be my firstborn, the most exalted of the kings of the earth. I will maintain my love to him forever, and my covenant with him will never fail. I will establish his line forever, his throne as long as the heavens endure. (Psalms 89:26-29).

Prince William is the elder son of King Charles III and is now first in line to the throne. He was fifteen when his mother, Princess Diana, died. Kate Middleton and Prince William got married in 2011. They had their first child, George, in July 2013, their second, Charlotte, in 2015, and their third, Louis, in 2018. William has inherited his father's Dutchy of Cornwall and is now the Prince of Wales. As heir to the throne, his main duties are to support the king in his royal commitments.

The line of succession identifies the sequence of members of the Royal Family in the order they stand in line as heir to the royal throne: Prince George is second in line to the throne, after his father. Charlotte Elizabeth Diana is third in line to the throne, after her father and older brother, and is known as Her Royal Highness Princess Charlotte of Wales. Then Louis Arthur Charles is fourth in line to the throne. It is a royal stipulation that the two heirs cannot travel on a flight together just in case something tragic were to happen. Once Prince George, who is second in line to the throne after Prince William, turns twelve, he will have to fly separately from his dad.

As it relates to God's Kingdom, I believe there is no line of succession and certainly no "Spare" just in case something terrible happens. God sent His only firstborn Son to be heir to His heavenly throne.

What then shall we say to all these things? If God is for us, who can be [successful] against us? He who did not spare [even] His own Son, but gave Him up for us all, how will He not also, along with Him, graciously give us all things? (Romans 8:31-32).

The heavenly Father, in His infinite wisdom, never needs a "SPARE." He gave us His only begotten Son as heir.

FIRSTBORN

This idea of firstborn is more than being first in line. It also describes superiority of position. King Charles III is the sovereign, and his heir-apparent is his first-born son, William, Prince of Wales. There are several places in the

New Testament that ascribe the status of 'firstborn' to Jesus. Think about this delightful passage, in which the apostle seems to magnify the sovereignty of Jesus as the firstborn and the exact visible image of God, the Father. Paul reminds us that Jesus Christ is the firstborn and the true sovereign above all other thrones:

He is the exact living image [the essential manifestation] of the unseen God [the visible representation of the invisible], the firstborn [the preeminent one, the sovereign, and the originator] of all creation." For by Him all things were created in heaven and on earth, [things] visible and invisible, whether thrones or dominions or rulers or authorities; all things were created and exist through Him [that is, by His activity] and for Him. And He Himself existed and is before all things, and in Him all things hold together. [His is the controlling, cohesive force of the universe.] (Colossians 1:15-20).

How can anyone ever read this passage and deny that Christ Jesus is not God's firstborn Son? Even before He was the first Son born to the Virgin Mary, he was the first-born Son of God, His heavenly Father. Surely, He was with God when all things were created, so He is the first to exist even before man existed. There is no prophet, king, or spiritual leader who can give you access to the throne of God. This wonderful and important psalm emphasizes God's promise to be with King David and his line forever:

He will call out to me, 'You are my Father, my God, the Rock my Saviour.' And I will appoint him to be my firstborn, the most exalted of the kings of the earth. I will maintain my love to him forever, and my covenant with him will never fail. I will establish his line forever, his throne as long as the heavens endure. (Psalms 89:26-29).

Can you hear the heart of King David crying to God, *"You are my Father, my God, and the Rock of my salvation!"* In David's cry, we perhaps also hear the cry of our hearts to Jesus, our Reigning King. Psalms 89 was written about real kings, often at special times like coronations or weddings or in perilous times when the king was in danger. However, the words of this psalm are no longer about earthly kings. Instead, the royal psalms had become about the promise of the Reigning King who was to come, the leader of God's future kingdom, pointing to Jesus, the Messiah. God promised David, *"I will set up your seed after you, who will come from your body, and I will establish his kingdom." (2 Samuel 7:12b).* This promise was partially fulfilled in Solomon, the direct son of David and immediate heir to his throne. It would be most perfectly fulfilled in the One known as the Son of David—the Messiah, Jesus Christ (see Matthew 12:23). The covenant God made with King David is also extended to his descendants and to the future generation of his linage to which Jesus was born. The Reigning King, Jesus Himself, will secure the rule of the Davidic dynasty forever.

Jesus is the sovereign "heir" of the Father, and we are His children. The certification and guarantee of our adoption is the indwelling of the Holy Spirit that unites us with Christ.

A better understanding of what it means to be an heir with Christ is depicted by Apostle Paul:

For you have not received a spirit of slavery leading again to fear [of God's judgment], but you have received the Spirit of adoption as sons [the Spirit producing sonship] by which we [joyfully] cry, "Abba! Father!" The Spirit Himself testifies and confirms together with our spirit [assuring us] that we [believers] are children of God. And if [we are His] children, [then we are His] heirs also: heirs of God and fellow heirs with Christ [sharing His spiritual blessing and inheritance], if indeed we share in His suffering so that we may also share in His glory. (Romans 8:15-17).

Being a co-heir with Christ means that we, as God's adopted children, will share in the inheritance of Jesus. What belongs to Jesus will also belong to us. The Word of God teaches that Christians should take hold of our position as heirs. Believers should rise up and become fruitful, multiply, dominate, subdue and replenish the earth, and inherit God's blessings as joint-heirs with Christ.

The term "heirs of God" emphasizes our relationship to God, the Father. As His children, we have "an inheritance that can never perish, spoil or fade . . . kept in heaven" (see 1 Peter 1:4). The Greek term translated "heirs" in Romans 8:17 refers to "those who receive their allotted possession by right of sonship." In other words, because God has made us His children (see John 1:12), we have full rights to receive His inheritance as His beneficiaries.

We are as welcome in God's family as Jesus is; we are *"accepted in the Beloved" (see Ephesians 1:6). "You are no longer a slave, but God's child; and since you are his child, God has made you also an heir." (Galatians 4:7).* Think of what that means. Everything God owns belongs to us as well because we belong to Him. Our eternal inheritance as co-heirs with Christ is the result of the blood of Jesus.

APPROACHING THE THRONE

With the Royal family, it is a biological bloodline. King Charles III inherits the throne as the firstborn son of the Queen, and Prince William is next in line as the firstborn son of His Father. Prince George will inherit the throne as the firstborn son of Prince William. Through the blood of Jesus, God made a covenant that whosoever believes in His firstborn Son will have access to His throne.

Therefore let us [with privilege] approach the throne of grace [that is, the throne of God's gracious favour] with confidence and without fear, so that we may receive mercy [for our failures] and find [His amazing] grace to help in time of need [an appropriate blessing, coming just at the right moment]. (Hebrews 4:16).

One of our greatest needs is to know that we can approach the throne of grace boldly as a child of God. Drawing near with confidence is a great invitation. For the kings of old, to approach the throne without being summoned was to be inviting death. You may recall Queen Esther's boldness: *"I will go to the king, though it is against the law, and if I perish, I perish." (Esther 4:16b).* Of course, Esther's confidence came from her trust in the sovereignty of God over life and death.

Our confidence comes because we are heirs of the Reigning King, who is perfect and sovereign over life and death. Drawing near with confidence to the throne of grace means this throne is unlike any other kind of throne. Many kings have been vicious tyrants; some others have been evil and deadly. There is no throne upon which a mortal king has sat that can be called a throne of grace. Our God is so gracious that He seats Himself upon it and surrounds Himself by it. His throne alone is a throne of grace. A guilty man coming before a king to beg for mercy does not come with confidence; he comes with wobbly knees and a trembling voice. But the confidence we have in drawing near the throne of grace is because we are children of God and heirs with the Reigning King. Not only is this one of the believers' greatest assurances, but the quality of the experience of being a son or daughter of God marks the relationship as the greatest of all privileges. To be able to call upon God as our heavenly Father because we are "in Christ" is the ultimate reason and meaning of our faith and the basis for meaningful Christian living.

We were not merely children who needed to mature; we had become enslaved to sin and needed to be redeemed—bought out of bondage—that we might enter the new family which Christ created by His death and resurrection. Adoption means both the redemption and the new relation of faith and trust in God. The adoption freed us from slavery to sonship and inheritance.

God's indwelling suggests a personal and intimate relationship. To be a child of God means that our heavenly Father dwells "in" His people by His Spirit. The indwelling presence of the living God demands a different, transformed life. To be a child of the King is to be blessed and beloved of God; yet there is no privilege without responsibility. Being God's child involves a sense of humility and duty. To be called a child of God carries with it discipline and consequences. As brothers and sisters in Christ, we are obligated to our Father, who bought us with the price of Christ's blood, to live our lives according to the guidance and control of His Spirit.

The duty of being a child of God is not to glorify self but to glorify Him who called us to be His own. The hope of life is based upon the assurance that we are the sons and daughters of God. The evidence of being a child of God is an awareness of the presence, leadership, and fellowship of the Holy Spirit. The peace of His presence provides confidence and hope that is beyond human understanding.

We approach the throne of God through prayer, and then His grace supplies all our needs according to His riches in glory. It is an amazing gift of grace from a God who is sovereign over all things and gives what we can never earn or deserve. We serve a great and mighty King, who invites us to enter His throne room with confidence by faith in the God who hears our prayer through Jesus, His Son.

The Father's house has many "rooms" or "mansions" and is a place of permanent dwelling. Revelation portrays a city of regal beauty: the holy Jerusalem, like a most precious stone, clear as crystal. The foundations of the wall of the city were adorned with numerous colourful stones (see Revelation 21:10-20).

Nothing can match the glory of this heavenly realm, and this is the mansion Jesus went to prepare with unlimited rooms for us. To abide in heaven is to fulfil one's purpose: living life in eternal devotion to and worship of Christ.

CHAPTER EIGHT
THE LAST WILL

And [I pray] that the eyes of your heart [the very centre and core of your being] may be enlightened [flooded with light by the Holy Spirit], so that you will know and cherish the hope [the divine guarantee, the confident expectation] to which He has called you, the riches of His glorious inheritance in the [saints (God's people), and [so that you will begin to know] what the immeasurable and unlimited and surpassing greatness of His [active, spiritual] power is in us who believe. (Ephesians 1:18-19).

When we think of an inheritance, we usually think about something a person receives from a relative or a friend who has died. The inheritance is given as part of the deceased's last will and testament. We are all familiar with inheritance. An inheritance is the passing of wealth and resources within the family from an elder to the younger. Sometimes it involves the death of the elder but not always. There are times when someone will pass on an inheritance while the beneficiaries are still alive. Inheritance is different from reward. A reward is based on merit or actions, while inheritance is generally based on relationship. I may receive a reward for good works, but most inheritances are received because we had a relationship with the giver.

ETERNAL INHERITANCE

In the Bible, the book of Hebrews tells us that because of Christ's death, all believers may receive the promised eternal inheritance. The "new covenant" in Christ is called the "last will and testament." That is why the Bible is separated into the Old Testament and the New Testament. God's last will is His Word, and studying the scriptures is the only way to know what we have inherited.

For this reason He is the Mediator and Negotiator of a new covenant [that is, an entirely new agreement uniting God and man], so that those who have been called [by God] may receive [the fulfilment of] the promised eternal inheritance, since a death has taken place [as the payment] which redeems them from the sins committed under the obsolete first covenant. For where there is a will and testament involved, the death of the one who made it must be established, for a will and testament takes effect [only] at death, since it is never in force as long as the one who made it is alive. So even the first covenant was not put in force without [the shedding of] blood." (Hebrews 9:15-18).

The will of God is our salvation and, ultimately, it is eternal life. It was from the will of God that the very thought of salvation was first planned. Had we been left to our own wills, we should have been separated from our heavenly Father. No man originated the idea of restoration for humanity. God Himself planned it before the foundations of the world, before the physical earth was created. It is His will that has brought those of us who are saved into the knowledge of the truth. This is the Father's will. Jesus said in John 6:38-40:

For I have come down from heaven, not to do My own will, but to do the will of Him who sent Me. This is the will of Him who sent Me, that of all that He has given Me I lose nothing, but that I [give new life and] raise it up at the last day. For this is My Father's will and purpose, that everyone who sees the Son and believes in Him [as Saviour] will have eternal life, and I will raise him up [from the dead] on the last day.

Christ is the divine executor of His Father's will, and the Holy Spirit is the witness and guarantor. When Christ forgives a sinner, it is His Father's will; when Christ, the Reigning King, receives us into His kingdom, it is His Father's will.

For the royal family, the Queen's written will is to remain hidden from the public for at least ninety years in line with a century-old tradition. The practice dates back to 1910, after the death of the grandmother of the late Queen. The will was kept under lock and key in a safe, which is under the care of a judge. Convention rules that the executor of their will applies to the head of the London High Court's Family Division for it to be sealed. A judge, who is the current president of the Family Division, is responsible for the safekeeping of the royal wills. He published the justification for the procedure following the death of Prince Philip aged 99 in 2021. The Queen had an estimated net worth of £370m in 2022, according to the Sunday Times rich list.

When the Queen sadly passed away on September 8, 2022, and King Charles III immediately succeeded her, the late monarch will no doubt have left a will. It is unlikely that the Queen's final will and testament will ever become public knowledge, with the wills of members of the royal family being sealed.

The will of God is divinely sealed by the blood of Jesus, so the will of God cannot be changed or unsealed. It is a fixed will, for God can never change His mind. His last and final will is the same from everlasting to everlasting and is not subject to change.

ABUNDANT INHERITANCE

The Father gave to the Son a kingdom of kings, priests, and saints who have washed their robes in the blood of the sinless, holy Lamb. I believe it was a number that no man can number, a number far beyond the bounds of our thought; but He did give a certain number whom He Himself had chosen from before the foundation of the world, and these became the property of the Lord Jesus Christ. They were put under a different government, being placed under the mediation of the Son of God. They became disciples—not by their own natural inclination, but by His gracious calling:

98

they became Christ's flock. He was their shepherd; they were to become Christ's body, He was to be the head; in due time they were to be Christ's bride, He was to be the husbandman.

The Lord's will is not simply gold and silver but the people whom He loves and has redeemed in Christ, and God delights in gathering us around Him to celebrate all the goodness of His abundant life.

"The Lord is the portion of my inheritance, my cup [He is all I need]; You support my lot. The [boundary] lines [of the land] have fallen for me in pleasant places; Indeed, my heritage is beautiful to me." (Psalm 16:5).

King David was the youngest son in a family with many older sons. He could expect no inheritance from his family, yet he took joy and comfort in the fact that God was the portion of his inheritance, and he knew that he had a good inheritance. The lines that marked out his inheritance had fallen to him in pleasant places.

Being born a British royal comes with life-long inheritance. The country's Sovereign Grant pays for housing, including mansions, wardrobe, and staff—and the staff gets outstanding benefits. King Charles III reportedly gets his shoelaces ironed and his toothbrush pasted. Queen Elizabeth had a valet who cleaned and polished her shoes.

God also promises inheritance. Israel inherited land as God's chosen children, even though they did not always act faithfully. We can understand how God is our inheritance because when we receive Christ, we become the beneficiaries of His great love. But for the Bible to say that we are God's inheritance—that is almost beyond belief. God, who owns everything in the universe, is thrilled that we are His possession. Therefore, the inheritance that the child of God receives is supernatural and abundant. What a contrast to our small gifts and legacies and benefits on this earth. Even the world's richest man can only leave what he has—nothing more. But God, being who He is, the inheritance we receive from Him is eternal and unlimited. There is more than enough inheritance for every person who accepts Jesus as their Saviour, Lord, and King.

Queen Elizabeth II sat on the throne for over seventy years, making her the longest-reigning British monarch in history. In that time, she amassed a huge fortune and many priceless possessions. So, now that she has passed, what does the Royal Family stand to inherit? Royal wills are not made public, so we will never know who inherited what except for the royal corgis; those will go to Prince Andrew.

The queen had an extensive personal tiara collection and jewelry that may be passed on to Princess Anne, her only daughter. King Charles III will inherit most of the late Sovereign's personal assets in its entirety. Likewise, our Reigning King Jesus has bestowed abundant wealth and inheritance upon us as kings and priests of the Father's Kingdom.

THE FATHER'S WEALTH

Everything in this universe belongs to God. He holds the exclusive rights and power to wealth. All the gold is His. All the silver is His. All the precious metals and jewels are His. All the land is His. All the animals are His. Everything material is His because it was all made from resources that belong to Him. Technically, the totality of the world's wealth belongs to God. All wealth comes from God, belongs to God, honours God, and is a blessing from God. When we accept that wealth is God's instead of ours, we are better equipped to manage it. Managing one's wealth calls for wisdom. We are called to honour God with all that we do, including the management of the wealth that He has so graciously bestowed.

Those who have gained wealth have also gained great responsibility to take care of that wealth, along with taking care of family, the church, and the less fortunate. This wealth is intended to provide for people, support ministries, feed the hungry, clothe the poor, help the helpless and protect the innocent. Those with Biblical wealth do not attach their self-worth to their net-worth but see their wealth as an opportunity to manage what God has blessed them with. We are not owners of our wealth, we are not owned by our wealth, and we are commanded to allow wealth to flow through us to bless others. We should view our wealth as a gift from God, entrusted to us, to carry out His work on earth. Wealth allows us to fund Kingdom business. Think of all the kingdom activities, such as church expansions, Christian schools and universities, missionaries, homeless shelters, medical missions, food banks, and children's homes. There is great contentment in being a part of the expansion of God's Kingdom.

God is not only the source and giver of all material things but the source of the immaterial as well. He is the source of life, and all that enriches life. He is the source of ability, grace, love, joy, peace, virtues of all kinds, family, spiritual vitality, growth, and hope. These belong to God and are His to distribute to whoever He wills.

In order for someone to receive an inheritance, a person has to have died. For us to receive "the promised eternal inheritance," Jesus died for our sake. The idea that inheritance is tied to death is a reality even with the royal family, lately with the death of the Queen. Now that Christ has died for us, He has established the new covenant in His blood so that we can receive "the promised eternal inheritance."

God chooses to share His wealth with His only Son, the Reigning King. Jesus came to earth to execute and decree God's will for whoever will believe in the New Covenant. The blood of Jesus, through His death on the cross, grants us free access to the throne of God; thereby, we can receive our kingdom inheritance.

I will declare the decree of the Lord: He said to Me, 'You are My Son; This day [I proclaim] I have begotten You. Ask of Me, and I will assuredly give [You] the nations as Your

inheritance, And the ends of the earth as Your possession.'
(Psalms 2:7-8).

In fact, part of the Holy Spirit's job is to help us understand all that has been freely given to us:

And [I pray] that the eyes of your heart [the very centre and core of your being] may be enlightened [flooded with light by the Holy Spirit], so that you will know and cherish the hope [the divine guarantee, the confident expectation] to which He has called you, the riches of His glorious inheritance in the [saints (God's people), and [so that you will begin to know] what the immeasurable and unlimited and surpassing greatness of His [active, spiritual] power is in us who believe. (Ephesians 1:18-19).

Now we have received, not the spirit of the world, but the Spirit who is from God, so that we may know the things freely given to us by God. All of us would like to leave a legacy of some sort to our children. It feels important enough to the giver and receiver to spend time doing it right. The Bible is not silent about inheritance. It addresses inheritance and leaving a legacy for our children. It has addressed both God's inheritance in us and ours in Him. God considers us a valuable gift as His special people.

He made known to us the mystery of His will according to His good pleasure, which He purposed in Christ, with regard to the fulfilment of the times [that is, the end of history, the climax of the ages]—to bring all things together in Christ, [both] things in the heavens and things on the

103

earth. In Him also we have [received an inheritance [a destiny—we were claimed by God as His own], having been predestined (chosen, appointed beforehand) according to the purpose of Him who works everything in agreement with the counsel and design of His will, so that we who were the first to hope in Christ [who first put our confidence in Him as our Lord and Saviour] would exist to the praise of His glory. In Him, you also, when you heard the word of truth, the good news of your salvation, and [as a result] believed in Him, were stamped with the seal of the promised Holy Spirit [the One promised by Christ] as owned and protected [by God]. The Spirit is the guarantee [the first instalment, the pledge, a foretaste] of our inheritance until the redemption of God's own [purchased] possession [His believers], to the praise of His glory. (Ephesians 1:9-14).

Paul shows us the awesome and wonderful word of truth to all believers. The apostle gives us a glimpse of the glorious blessings God has planned for and promised to those who come to Him through His Son, Jesus Christ. The contents of our heavenly Father's will meant that we were elected, or predestined before the world or time existed. We have been redeemed in this present age, and we will receive our complete inheritance in the ages to come.

CHAPTER NINE
THE KING'S GIFTS

After hearing the king, they went their way; and behold, the star, which they had seen in the east, went on before them [continually leading the way] until it came and stood over the place where the young Child was. When they saw the star, they rejoiced exceedingly with great joy. And after entering the house, they saw the Child with Mary His mother; and they fell down and worshiped Him. Then, after opening their treasure chests, they presented to Him gifts [fit for a king, gifts] of gold, frankincense, and myrrh. (Matthew 2:9-11).

Many Christmas carols make mention of the three kings who followed a star and came to pay homage to baby Jesus in Bethlehem. The Bible speaks of Magi, or wise men, who followed a star from the East to Bethlehem in search of a newborn king. There they found Mary and baby Jesus and offered Him gifts of gold, frankincense, and myrrh.

Their gifts had special symbolic meanings: gold signified Jesus' status as "King," frankincense represented the divinity and identity as the Son of God; and myrrh is symbolic of Jesus' humanity.

Millions of Christmas cards show three kings presenting gifts to a tiny child in a manger. People sing "We Three Kings of Orient Are." The fact that so little information is given about the wise men clearly shows that Matthew's interest was not focused on the wise men themselves. Rather, he was interested in the fact that people came to worship the Reigning King with gifts. Let us draw special attention to the gifts Jesus received.

GOLD

It is easy to see why gold is an appropriate gift for Jesus Christ. Gold always starts with God. If we add the letter "l" (for love) to the word "God," we get the word "gold." Gold is the metal of kings because it has great value which is highly desired. Jesus is precious, and His promises are precious. His value far exceeds the value of all the gold that can be found in the universe.

When gold was presented to Jesus, it acknowledged His right to rule and reign. The wise men knew Jesus was the King of kings. When gold is uncovered on earth, it is not in the desirable condition that jewelers are looking for. The gold must be refined so impurities float to the top for removal, leaving only the pure gold behind.

The gold that John saw in heaven was of such quality that it appeared to be transparent to reflect the pure light of God's blazing glory. God's ability to purify is not confined only to gold; God has purified all who will enter His heaven through the blood of Jesus Christ.

"If we [freely] admit that we have sinned and confess our sins, He is faithful and just [true to His own nature and promises], and will forgive our sins and cleanse us continually from all unrighteousness [our wrongdoing, everything not in conformity with His will and purpose] (1 John 1:9).

Think for a moment about how gold is found and processed. It is similar to the way God purifies us from all our sins. Our attention in eternity will hardly be focused on earthly treasures because we are cleansed and purified by the shed blood of Jesus. While man pursues treasures like gold on earth, one day, it will simply be no more than a source of pavement for the believer in heaven. No matter how many precious jewels or materials make up the splendour of heaven, nothing will ever be of greater value and more golden than our heavenly Father who loves us. Forsaking the gold of this world, our desire should always be for the golden riches of God's love.

In ancient days, kings were adorned with gold to signify their high position. They were also given gifts of gold to pay homage to their position. Of course, they surrounded themselves with items of gold to proclaim their wealth. The wealth of this world will never satisfy. Ezekiel 7:19 says:

...their silver and their gold shall not be able to deliver them in the day of the wrath of the Lord: they [silver and gold] shall not satisfy their souls.

King Solomon had an ivory throne overlaid with the best gold (see 1 Kings 10:18). When instructions were given for building the furniture in the tabernacle, God was very specific about the use of gold. Every piece of furniture pointed to Christ and to His deity. For example, in the holy of holies, the Ark of the Covenant was constructed of acacia wood (symbolic of Jesus' humanity) and overlaid with pure gold (symbolic of His divinity). The mercy seat was pure gold as well as the two cherubim, one on each side with wings outstretched (see Exodus 25:10-21). The lampstand was constructed of pure gold, and the table of shewbread and the altar of incense were constructed of acacia wood (Christ's humanity) and overlaid with gold (Christ's divinity). Gold symbolizes royalty and the right of King Jesus Christ to rule and reign in our lives.

INCENSE

Frankincense was also a significant gift. Incense was used in the temple worship. It was mixed with the oil that was used to anoint the priests of Israel. It was part of the meal offerings that were offerings of thanksgiving and praise to God. In presenting this gift, the wise men pointed to Christ as our great High Priest, the one whose whole life was acceptable and well-pleasing to His Father.

Our prayers to God are like the sweet smell of incense to Him. David writes in Psalm 141:2. *"Let my prayer be counted as incense before You; The lifting up of my hands as the evening offering."*

The altar of incense symbolised the sacrifices and prayers that ascended to God on behalf of Israel. It was a reminder to the people that prayer was to play a central role in their relationship with God. God instructed how the incense should be made: from the resin and gums of certain trees and other products. When it was burned, it gave off a fragrant aroma which would then float around the inside and outside of the temple. When the people smelt it, they would know that their prayers were continuously going up to God as the incense was burnt day and night. According to Exodus 30:1-31:18, prayer is our incense to God instead of burnt offerings and sacrifices.

We no longer need to burn the incense, but we do need to offer up our prayers to our heavenly Father in Jesus' name. God gives us the privilege to pray. He starts the fire within us, and we respond by praying His desires back to Him. Prayer begins with the instructions from God's Word.

THE INGREDIENT OF SALT

Salt was one of the ingredients to be mixed with the spices to make some incense. That is why Jesus refers to us as being the salt of the earth.

On one occasion, Queen Elizabeth II was given a bag of rocks by the governor of the British Virgin Islands. The gift was a symbolic nod to 'the tradition of the British Virgin Islands as a tax on the production of minerals on Salt Island, one of the islands in the Caribbean region.' Salt was one of her strangest gifts to date.

Salt makes food taste better, either by adding flavour to something that would otherwise be bland, by enhancing flavours that are already there or by providing a contrast with a very different sort of taste. These are probably the uses of salt that most of us think of. They are a powerful illustration of the way Christians are to serve the world. We are intended to spread throughout the world and enhance it, adding flavour to things that would be bland, drawing out the blessings of whatever is good, and providing a contrast by being distinct and different. Paul tells us to ensure that our speech is *"seasoned with salt, so that you may know how you ought to answer each person" (Colossians 4:6).*

Salt was the ancient equivalent of refrigeration. If you wanted to stop meat or fish from decaying, you could rub in salt and preserve it for longer. This was the main reason salt was so valuable. Roman soldiers were sometimes paid in salt, which is the origin of our word "salary." Disciples of Jesus, in this sense, are sent into the world to keep it from decay, preserving its goodness and preventing it from becoming corrupted or ruined, which is a helpful thing to bear in mind as we go to work every day. Salt does not just savour; it saves.

The earthly high priest accepts the incense offering to God on the altar, with salt as one of the main ingredients. Likewise, Jesus accepts the gifts of incense from us in the form of our salted prayers and forever intercedes to God on our behalf.

MYRRH

Myrrh was used for embalming. By any human imagination, it would be peculiar to present to the infant Christ a spice used for embalming, but it was a gift of faith. We do not know precisely what the wise men may have known or guessed about Christ's ministry, but we do know that the Old Testament repeatedly foretold His suffering. Myrrh is not only a symbol of Christ's death but also of the spiritual death that covers you because of your sin. Lay it at Christ's feet, saying, *"Lord Jesus Christ, I know that I am less perfect than You are and am a sinner. I know that I should receive the consequence of my sin, which is to be separated from Your presence forever, but You took my sin, dying in my place. I believe that. Now I ask You to accept me as Your child forever."* Unlike the Israelites—whose sins were only covered by the blood of the animal sacrifices—our sins are removed forever due to the sacrifice of Jesus.

After you have done that, come with your incense, acknowledging that your life is as impure as the life of the Lord Jesus Christ is sinless. The Bible teaches that Christ comes to live in us as His followers so that our life may become the fragrance of Christ.

For we are the sweet fragrance of Christ [which ascends] to God, [discernible both] among those who are being saved and among those who are perishing; to the latter one an aroma from death to death [a fatal, offensive odor], but to the other an aroma from life to life [a vital fragrance, living and fresh]. And who is adequate and sufficiently qualified for these things? (2 Corinthians 2:15-16).

Jesus, as we know, loved using everyday items to communicate truths about God and His people. As followers of Jesus, the gifts the wise men delivered are symbolic of the gifts we carry as we all have a peculiar role to play as God's kingdom comes on earth.

According to the New York Times, during a visit to the Persian Gulf in 1979, the Queen and the late Duke of Edinburgh were gifted with 'millions of dollars' worth of gifts by their hosts. The presents included a royal ransom of jewels, carpets and gold coffee jugs, incense burners, handbags, gold swords, a glittering knee-length apron, and an 18-inch-tall solid gold palm tree studded with pearls. The Queen was reported to have been 'stunned' by the generosity and lavish standards of the gifts.

On the Queen's 18th birthday, she was given a gift that would surely ignite her love of dogs for the rest of her life. Her father, King George VI, presented his daughter with a corgi puppy named Susan to mark the occasion. Susan was the first of a long line of corgis owned by Her Majesty, all of them descended from her first pet. Also, in a rare gesture of generosity, the Kingdom of Jordan gave the monarch a ceramic figure of her son, Prince Charles, alongside the cartoon character, Postman Pat, in honour of Her Majesty's 90th birthday.

God bestows upon all members of His church in every age spiritual gifts that each member uses for the common good of the church and humanity. These spiritual gifts help us to be faithful stewards of God's Kingdom through the gift of grace. The church represents God's Kingdom, and we should all bring our gifts to the Reigning King in order that they can be accepted in faith and love.

CHAPTER TEN
GOD SAVE THE KING

And there is salvation in no one else; for there is no other name under heaven that has been given among people by which we must be saved [for God has provided the world no alternative for salvation]. (Acts 4:12).

The song "God Save the King" was first performed publicly in London in 1745, which came to be known as the National Anthem at the beginning of the nineteenth century. Additional verses have been added down the years, but these are rarely used. On official occasions, only the first verse is usually sung, substituting "Queen" for "King" where appropriate. The words of the National Anthem are as follows:

God save our gracious King! Long live our noble King! God save the King! Send him victorious, happy, and glorious, long to reign over us, God save the King. Thy choicest gifts in store, on him be pleased to pour, long may he reign. May he defend our laws, and ever give us cause, to sing with heart and voice, GOD SAVE THE KING.

For the first time in over seventy years, following the accession of Charles III, 'God Save the King' was sung in public as the national and royal anthem of the United Kingdom and many Commonwealth nations. It resounded at a memorial service for the late, beloved Queen Elizabeth II at St. Paul's Cathedral on Friday, September 9, 2022, and once more the following day when Charles III was proclaimed King in front of the Accession Council at St. James's Palace in London.

'God Save the Queen,' in the words of the British national anthem, is so familiar to audiences in concert halls, cathedrals, sports stadiums, and public events across the country, but the queen's version may not be heard again. As the national anthem reverts to its original version, following the death of Her Majesty Queen Elizabeth II, crowds gathered outside Buckingham Palace to sing both 'God Save the Queen' in memory of Her Majesty, and 'God Save the King' for Charles III. 'God Save the King' had not been sung publicly since 1952 when Elizabeth's father, George VI, died. From now on, it will be heard as the national anthem of the United Kingdom and the Commonwealth at all appropriate royal occasions and sporting events.

PUBLIC PROCLAMATION

Salvation is a celebrated experience in personal testimonies, as in so many Psalms, traditional hymns, and worship songs.

In a public declaration of the faith, in seasons of worldwide celebrations, and in times of corporate worship, we should continue to pray earnestly for the salvation of earthly kings. The words of truth in this well-known Christmas Carol declare that the Saviour Reigns:

Joy to the world, the Lord is come!
Let earth receive her King;
Let every heart prepare Him room
And heaven and nature sing
And heaven and nature sing
And heaven, and heaven, and nature sing

Joy to the world, the Savior reigns!
Let men their songs employ;
While fields and floods, rocks, hills and plains
Repeat the sounding joy
Repeat the sounding joy
Repeat, repeat, the sounding joy

No more let sins and sorrows grow
Nor thorns infest the ground;
He comes to make His blessings flow
Far as the curse is found
Far as the curse is found
Far as, far as the curse is found

He rules the world with truth and grace
And makes the nations prove
The glories of His righteousness
And wonders of His love
And wonders of His love
And wonders, wonders, of His love

Indeed, all of nature celebrates our Saviour and King; yes, He rules with truth and grace. We will continue to repeat the sounding joy and sing of the wonders of His love. The atoning joy of salvation that Jesus brings to this world allows His Kingdom blessings to flow into our lives instead of the infestation of the curse. This assurance calls for celebration at this present time as we witness all the turmoil that is taking place in the world around us: the ongoing war in Ukraine, the aftermath of the global pandemic, financial crisis, and poverty around the world. Added to this, we have unstable leadership in government, violence, fraud, immoral lifestyles, and more, all evident in society. These things make it abundantly clear to us that the world we live in is filled with sin and is desperately in need of God's forgiveness and mercy.

In proclaiming Jesus as Saviour of the world, we agree that He is the only Way, the Truth, and the Life. To recognize Jesus as the Saviour of the world is to believe that if anyone in the world is saved, it is only in and through His name:

And there is salvation in no one else; for there is no other name under heaven that has been given among people by which we must be saved [for God has provided the world no alternative for salvation]. (Acts 4:12).

In the scriptures, we see that "God saves" covers a huge range of experiences and circumstances in which God's saving power rescues and delivers people through human history. God saves people in a practical way, resulting in forgiveness, mercy, healing, deliverance, victory, and triumph, but God's salvation goes much further. The Bible recognizes that all evils from which God saves His people originated from the sinful nature of the human heart. That is where the deepest source of the problems lies. There is, therefore, a need for God to deal with sin—sin in the world and sin in every person.

BEHOLD THE LAMB OF GOD

Lifting his hand and pointing to Jesus, John the Baptist proclaimed, *"Look! The Lamb of God who takes away the sin of the world." (John 1:29)*. He saw Christ as the perfect sacrifice for our sins. He did not say, "Behold the great king" or "Behold the Son of God." Although, both these honours are true, but the first salutation with such assurance was, "Behold the Lamb of God."

No earthly king can save themselves, so we should sing the British National Anthem by faith and with a prayerful petition, "God Save the King." We must believe that Christ is the Saviour of the world and no one who denies Him will be saved. To offer salvation apart from Christ is to offer false hope. The way that Jesus saved the world is by making an atonement for our sins to be forgiven. When Jesus was crucified, that one death that He died on the cross at Calvary was sufficient to take away the sins of humanity. That is what the Bible says in 1 John 2:2:

And He is the propitiation for our sins: and not for ours only, but also for the sins of the whole world. (KJV).

119

We believe, of course, that Christ's death ultimately saves us from the death penalty of sin.

For the wages of sin is death, but the free gift of God [that is, His remarkable, overwhelming gift of grace to believers] is eternal life in Christ Jesus our Lord. (Romans 6:23).

Sin has been multiplying in this world ever since the time that the first man fell into sin. Even from the time a person is born, he already has a sinful nature. Since all men are born in sin, we all fall short of God's glory:

Since all have sinned and continually fall short of the glory of God, and are being justified [declared free of the guilt of sin, made acceptable to God, and granted eternal life] as a gift by His [precious, undeserved] grace, through the redemption [the payment for our sin] which is [provided] in Christ Jesus, whom God displayed publicly [before the eyes of the world] as a [life-giving] sacrifice of atonement and reconciliation (propitiation) by His blood [to be received] through faith. This was to demonstrate His righteousness [which demands punishment for sin], because in His forbearance [His deliberate restraint] He passed over the sins previously committed [before Jesus' crucifixion]. It was to demonstrate His righteousness at the present time, so that He would be just and the One who justifies those who have faith in Jesus [and rely confidently on Him as Saviour]. (Romans 3:23-26).

We can now see that the greatest need in the world today is not for financial stability or for lower mortgage rates, new religious movements, or anything else. Neither is it for more scientific research to find a vaccine for infectious illnesses like the COVID-19 outbreak that spread worldwide. We must recognise that these are symptoms indicating that we need something more powerful and everlasting. Only God can deal with the source of all the world's problems. What we need most is God's salvation from SIN! Without dealing with this root cause of all evil, found in the hearts of men, any attempt to change the world will prove worthless. Only Jesus is worthy to save the world.

GOD SAVE THE QUEEN!

Regardless of what you think of the monarchy, no one can deny that Queen Elizabeth was a remarkable woman. Not only was she the longest-serving monarch in history, but she lived through more change than any other royal and managed to handle it surprisingly well. Throughout it all, the Queen acknowledged that her faith in Jesus had been a significant source of strength amidst the grueling demands and pressures of this role that was thrust upon her.

Queen Elizabeth II held the title "Defender of the Faith and Supreme Governor of the Church of England," but for the seven decades of her monarchy, these were not mere titles. Many have spoken of her deep Christian faith and how she lived it. The Queen often spoke openly and with conviction about her deep faith during her ninety-six years of life. Her Christian faith and personal relationship with Jesus has been an answered prayer:

"God save our gracious Queen! God Save the Queen."

Indeed, only God can save us all, not just the Queen and King. God's Word says that we are saved by grace through faith in Christ Jesus and not by our own efforts or works (see Ephesians 2:8-9). Grace alone. Faith alone.

Grace alone means that God loves, forgives, and saves us not because of who we are or what we do but because of the work of Christ. Our best efforts can never be good enough to earn salvation, but God declares us righteous for Christ's sake. God even gives us the faith to trust Him. In fact, the entire Royal family cannot be saved by charitable deeds, wealth, or years of service, but by grace through faith in Christ. Our salvation is in God's hands. That is good news: the gospel. We are invited to live out our faith with thankful hearts, eager to share the gospel with others.

It should be remembered that at the time of Jesus' crucifixion, two thieves were punished beside Him (see Luke 23:33–43), and on the cross, one of the men rejected Jesus by mocking and blaspheming Him (see Matthew 27:44; Mark 15:32), as did many of the spectators. One of the thieves responded in faith to the message of salvation and was granted access to the Kingdom of God and entered paradise that very day.

Because salvation belongs to our God, it is experienced on our side through the "cry for help." If we have found Him to be the one who hears our prayers, then we have a reason for worship and celebration. The salvation of God is for those who call on Him, fear Him, cry to Him, and love Him. Everywhere in the New Testament, of course, salvation is offered by God's grace only through repentance and faith. We experience salvation by receiving it, not by achieving it. Everybody is desperate for salvation, since we are all hopeless and caught up in our own nature and actions. Each one of us needs the victory that is found in Jesus Christ.

What we learn from the saved thief on the cross is that we are all sinners in need of a Saviour, and no matter if we think our sins are trivial or terrible, it is never too late to repent and accept the free gift of salvation. This gift of salvation is received when you open your heart to accept forgiveness and cleansing from the heart by the Holy Spirit. If you have a mind and the will to choose life over death, it is not too late to receive the gospel by faith.

THE CHRISTMAS MESSAGES

Queen Elizabeth II's Christmas broadcast became a part of Christmas festivities both in the United Kingdom and the Commonwealth. Following the first Christmas Broadcast given by King George V in 1932, his granddaughter, Queen Elizabeth II, continued the tradition using the medium of radio, television and, more recently, the internet, to speak directly to the public. She embraced advances in technology to deliver the broadcast, and 2012 was the first year in which viewers could watch the queen in 3D. Despite these changes, the Queen's message during the broadcast always sought to reaffirm the core values of human kindness and interaction, not just at Christmas but at all times of the year. The established Christmas tradition provided an opportunity for the Queen to communicate her reflections about events that have unfolded over the course of the year and her hopes for the future both in the United Kingdom and the Commonwealth.

The Queen gave her first Christmas message ten months after she became sovereign, but before she was officially crowned. She paid tribute to her "beloved" late father and reflected on her accession to the throne. Asking them to pray for her ahead of her coronation, she wrote "You will be keeping it as a holiday, but I want to ask you all, whatever your religion may be, to pray for me that day." Faith played a key role in the Queen's public and private life. We take a closer look at one of her most cherished hymns:

Praise, my soul, the King of heaven; To his feet your tribute bring. Ransomed, healed, restored, forgiven, evermore his praises sing. Alleluia, alleluia! Praise the everlasting King! Praise him for his grace and favour, To his people in distress. Praise him, still the same as ever, slow to chide, and swift to bless. Alleluia, alleluia! Glorious in his faithfulness!

Fatherlike, he tends and spares us; well our feeble frame he knows. In his hand he gently bears us, rescues us from all our foes. Alleluia, alleluia! Widely yet his mercy flows! Angels, help us to adore him; You behold him face to face. Sun and moon, bow down before him, dwellers all in time and space. Alleluia, alleluia! Praise with us the God of grace!

124

Our English word "praise" comes from the old French term "preisier," which means "to prize." When we think about it, we can see the relationship between the Queen and Jesus. Before we can praise anything, we must first come to know and place a high value on it. We can only praise what we honour and value. Although the Queen had experienced great wealth and owned many things of great value, she did not praise them over her everlasting King. The Queen honoured the King of Heaven. How perfectly the above song relates to us praising Jesus. Without first knowing Him intimately and personally, we cannot adequately respect and worship Him. Since the Messiah has died for our sins and has changed our lives, we should say so: "Praise, my soul, the King of heaven; To his feet your tribute bring. Ransomed, healed, restored, forgiven, evermore his praises sing. Alleluia, alleluia! Praise the everlasting King!"

Back to the National Anthem:

God save the King! Send him victorious, happy, and glorious, long to reign over us, God save the King.

Let the nations join in this sung prayer; let the church resound this with spiritual discernment and understanding. Let us call on Jesus, the Reigning King, to reign over us and save King Charles III. Send him your victory; God save the King!

CHAPTER ELEVEN
THE KING'S CORONATION

And I looked, and behold a white cloud, and upon the cloud one sat like unto the son of man, having on his head a golden crown, and in his hand a sharp sickle. (Revelation 14:14 – KJV).

One of the major events in any monarchy is the crowning of the new king. Buckingham Palace has announced that the Coronation of His Majesty the King will take place on Saturday, May 6, 2023. The Coronation ceremony will take place at Westminster Abbey, London, and will be conducted by the Archbishop of Canterbury. The ceremony will see His Majesty King Charles III crowned alongside the Queen Consort.

The coronation is a religious service that requires the king to take an oath before his country. At these royal ceremonies, there is usually splendour everywhere, extravagant clothing, jewels, horses, carriages, archbishops, and famous dignitaries from the nations. Everything points to the glory of the individual being crowned, His Majesty.

A coronation is a ceremony marking the formal inauguration of a monarch with royal power. At the age of eleven, Princess Elizabeth had watched her father, King George VI, crowned in the elaborate ceremony. The Queen succeeded to the throne on February 6, 1952 on the death of her father, King George VI. She was in Kenya at the time, and on June 2, 1953, sixteen months later, her own official coronation took place.

King Charles III officially became King on Thursday, September 8, when his mother, Queen Elizabeth II, passed away at Balmoral in Scotland. Every king is crowned in a coronation ceremony. A coronation is the placement or conferral of a crown upon a sovereign's head. The concepts of royalty, coronation, and deity are linked.

KING JESUS

Jesus Christ is no exception. He too will be crowned as the Reigning King. In the book of revelation, Jesus is given the full title "KING OF KINGS AND LORD OF LORDS" (see Revelation 17:14). The title indicates someone who has the power to exercise absolute dominion over all His realms. In the case of the Lord Jesus, the realm is all of creation. In John's vision, Jesus is returning to judge the world and establish His Kingdom. In the Bible, we find a coronation for the reigning of a King, and He is affirmed as a King, and He is inaugurated into His Kingship.

Jesus rides on a donkey into His capital city as a conquering King and is hailed by the people. The streets of Jerusalem—the royal city—held a royal procession, and like a king, He ascended to His palace, not a temporal palace, but the spiritual palace of His Father's kingdom. The spreading of cloaks was an act of homage for royalty. Jesus was openly declaring to the people that He was their King and the Messiah they had been waiting for.

The next day, when the large crowd who had come to the Passover feast heard that Jesus was coming to Jerusalem, they took branches of palm trees [in homage to Him as King] and went out to meet Him, and they began shouting and kept shouting "Hosanna! Blessed (celebrated, praised) is He who comes in the name of the Lord, even the King of Israel!"
And Jesus, finding a young donkey, sat on it; just as it is written [in Scripture], "Do not fear, Daughter of Zion; Behold, Your King is coming, seated on a donkey's colt. His disciples did not understand [the meaning of] these things at first; but when Jesus was glorified and exalted, they remembered that these things had been written about Him and had been done to Him. (John 12:12-16).

The people who were celebrating Jesus' arrival in Jerusalem were quoting Psalm 118:25-26, *O Lord, save now, we beseech You; O Lord, we beseech You, send now prosperity and give us success! Blessed is the one who comes in the name of the Lord; We have blessed you from the house of the Lord [you who come into His sanctuary under His guardianship].*

The phrase "save us" is the same as "Hosanna." You probably have seen palm branches hanging as ornaments on doors and windows around the season of Easter. This is because a palm branch is the most significant symbol on Palm Sunday. Its origin can be traced back to a vivid Jewish tradition and Christian history. In history, the palm branch symbolizes the triumph and victory of the life of Jesus Christ who forever changed the world.

According to the New York Times, during a visit to the Persian Gulf in 1979, the Queen and the Duke of Edinburgh were gifted with an 18-inch-tall solid gold palm tree studded with pearls. Today, various Christian churches still use the palm branch as a symbol of God's victory and power.

Visual palm branches signify the victory and triumph Jesus has over death, and was significant in the celebration of Jesus Christ's triumphal entry into Jerusalem. Each one of us needs the victory that is found in Jesus Christ. This victory is freely ours if we live by faith. Claiming this victory will give us freedom from sin, guilt, shame, and death. We can overcome the enemy's schemes and deception through the blood of Christ. Death lost its sting when Jesus rose again with the victor's crown on His head. We celebrate this success with palm branches to remind us of this victory as a token of triumph.

The palm tree is an important symbol of victory for Israel after God delivered the Israelites from slavery in Egypt. After Israel got out of Egypt, the Lord commanded that they celebrate a feast in honour of the freedom they had from the hands of their captors who enslaved them for hundreds of years. The celebration is never complete without the waving and decorations of palm branches.

After these things I looked, and this is what I saw: a vast multitude which no one could count, [gathered] from every nation and from all the tribes and peoples and languages [of the earth], standing before the throne and before the Lamb (Christ), dressed in white robes, with palm branches in their hands; and in a loud voice they cried out, saying, "Salvation [belongs] to our God who is seated on the throne, and to the Lamb [our salvation is the Trinity's to give, and to God the Trinity we owe our deliverance]." And all the angels were standing around the throne and around the [twenty-four] elders and the four living creatures; and they fell to their faces before the throne and worshiped God, saying, "Amen! Blessing and glory and majesty and wisdom and thanksgiving and honour and power and might belong to our God forever and ever. Amen." (Revelation 7:9-12).

Imagine what it would be like for you to be shown the heavenly glory of the saints that Christ purchased by His blood, and to be shown the glorious coronation that would take place with the saints singing "Salvation belongs to our God who is seated on the throne," waving palm branches in their hands. No royal procession ever seen on earth, or no coronation of any earthly king, can match this glory and majesty of heaven.

CROWNS

A crown is a symbolic headgear that is worn by a monarch or deity. It is a very powerful symbol of authority and power. The Greek word translated "crown" is "stephanos," and means "a badge of royalty, a prize in the public games or a symbol of honour." It can be described as a wreath or garland of leaves placed on a victor's head as a reward for winning an athletic contest. A crown represents victory, majesty, power, and sovereignty. In the Kingdom of God, crowns are heavenly rewards that God promises to those who are faithful. As mentioned in the New Testament, there are many imperishable crowns that will be awarded to believers.

A crown was made for Queen Victoria in 1838. The crown was made out of precious rubies and sapphires. In the middle of it was a 309-carat diamond. On June 2, 1953, the Archbishop of Canterbury placed St. Edward's Crown on the head of Queen Elizabeth II. When the Archbishop of Canterbury crowns King Charles III, he will place St. Edward's Crown on the monarch's head. This will be the first and only time that Charles will wear this specific crown. It is exceptionally heavy, but it has been worn by all monarchs over the past century—George V, George VI, and Elizabeth II—at the moment of their crowning. Before the end of the coronation ceremony, St. Edward's crown is swapped for the lighter and slightly more comfortable Imperial State Crown. That is the one we are all more familiar with, as the late Queen wore it for decades at the annual State Opening of Parliament. It is also the crown that rested on her coffin after her death.

Revelation 4:1-4 says:

After this I looked, and there before me was a door standing open in heaven. And the voice I had first heard speaking to me like a trumpet said, "Come up here, and I will show you what must take place after this." At once I was in the Spirit, and there before me was a throne in heaven with someone sitting on it. And the one who sat there had the appearance of jasper and ruby. A rainbow that shone like an emerald encircled the throne. Surrounding the throne were twenty-four other thrones and seated on them were twenty-four elders. They were dressed in white and had crowns of gold on their heads.

Christ was never crowned King of kings by men while He walked this earth because God had reserved His heavenly crown until the day He ascended to the throne. The coronation ceremony of Jesus takes place in the heavenly realms before the throne of God where the elders were envisioned by John wearing golden crowns.

"From the throne came flashes of lightning, rumblings, and peals of thunder. In front of the throne, seven lamps were blazing. These are the seven spirits of God. Also in front of the throne there was what looked like a sea of glass, clear as crystal. In the centre, around the throne, were four living creatures, and they were covered with eyes, in front and in back. The first living creature was like a lion, the second was

like an ox, the third had a face like a man, the fourth was like a flying eagle. Each of the four living creatures had six wings and was covered with eyes all around, even under its wings. Day and night they never stop saying: "Holy, holy, holy is the Lord God Almighty, who was, and is, and is to come." Whenever the living creatures give glory, honour and thanks to him who sits on the throne and who lives for ever and ever, the twenty-four elders fall before him who sits on the throne and worship him who lives for ever and ever. They lay their crowns before the throne and say: "You are worthy, our Lord and God, to receive glory and honour and power, for you created all things, and by your will they were created and have their being." (Revelation 4:5-11).

God's throne is in heaven, so that is where the coronation of Jesus as the reigning King takes place. No place on earth is holy enough to host such a solemn occasion. Our two physical ears, our deficient eyes, and our imperfect hearts could not contain the flashes of lighting, the mighty sound of thunder, and the fire from the blazing lamps. The response from the elders tells the awesomeness of the sovereign coronation orchestrated by Almighty God. He alone is worthy to receive all glory, honour, and praise as the Creator of all things. This was revealed even before Christ's first coming.

Daniel describes the scene in these words:

I kept looking until thrones were set up, and the Ancient of Days took His seat; His vesture was like white snow, and the hair of His head like pure wool. His throne was ablaze with flames, its wheels were a burning fire. A river of fire was flowing and coming out from before Him; thousands upon thousands were attending Him, and myriads upon myriads were standing before Him; the court sat, and the books were opened. (Daniel 7:9-10).

No earthly throne can compare with the blazing fiery seats of the heavenly throne room. What a setting for the coronation of the great King—the exaltation of King Jesus seated on the throne? The writer of Hebrews writes, *"When He had made purification of sins, He sat down at the right hand of the Majesty on high." (Hebrews 1:3b).*

I saw in the night visions, and, behold, one like the Son of man came with the clouds of heaven, and came to the Ancient of days, and they brought him near before him. And there was given him dominion, and glory, and a kingdom, that all people, nations, and languages, should serve him: his dominion is an everlasting dominion, which shall not pass away, and his kingdom that which shall not be destroyed. (Daniel 7:13-14).

Jesus Christ must return to this world as King of kings to establish God's government. Jesus Christ's message was to preach the Kingdom of God. This is the gospel He brought: the good news of eternity. Jesus will return to fulfil His office as "King of kings." We see in Revelation 14:14 that Christ will have a golden crown on His head. This symbol will designate Him as supreme King over all nations. The Reigning King will come with great power, and God's government will rule in justice, faithfulness, and truth.

THE LION OF JUDAH

Often, when we think of Jesus, one of the images that come to mind is the lamb portraying tenderness, gentleness, and submissiveness. Let us consider the significance of the tribe of Judah. Judah was one of the twelve sons of Jacob. To make it simple, the descendants of these sons formed the twelve tribes of Israel. A reference to the tribe of Judah is a reference to the human or natural lineage of Christ. Jesus was a descendant of Judah, which also included David.

In Genesis 49, lions were mentioned when Jacob calls his sons together and tells them what will happen to each of them in the days to come. Clearly, Jacob is speaking with prophetic language. When he gets to his son Judah, here is what he proclaims:

Judah, your brothers will praise you; your hand will be on the neck of your enemies; your father's sons will bow down to you. You are a lion's cub, Judah; you return from the prey, my son. Like a lion he crouches and lies down, like a lioness—who dares to rouse him? The sceptre will not depart from Judah, nor the ruler's staff from between his feet, until he to whom it belongs shall come and the obedience of the nations shall be his. He will tether his donkey to a vine, his colt to the choicest branch; he will wash his garments in wine, his robes in the blood of grapes. His eyes will be darker than wine, his teeth whiter than milk. (Genesis 49:8-12).

When you consider these verses, the Lion of the tribe of Judah points to the conquering, victorious King that would descend from Judah's lineage. We know the lion is only one person, Jesus Himself. He is the Lion of the tribe of Judah. The enemy is like a roaring lion, but he has no power over the greatest Lion. Lions are legendary for their strength, beauty, and fearlessness. Jesus is called the Lion of Judah because He has triumphed over temptation and sin, over pain and suffering, over fear, death, and even over the devil himself.

Then the end will come, when he hands over the kingdom to God the Father after he has destroyed all dominion, authority and power. For he must reign until he has put all his enemies under his feet. The last enemy to be destroyed is death. For he 'has put everything under his feet.' (1 Corinthians 15:24-26).

Our Lion has given us victory over sin and has removed the penalty of death and replaced it with the promise and hope of eternal life. You can celebrate because you are victorious today. You are no longer under the penalty of sin. The lion character enlarges our understanding of baby Jesus in the manger, the suffering Saviour on the cross, and a deeper revelation of Jesus as the conquering King of kings. When Daniel was thrown into the lion's den, he could not be destroyed because the conquering Lion was evidently there with him. God showed His authority over even the most powerful of beasts that He Himself created by shutting the lions' mouths. Daniel emerged from the den victorious, and the enemies acknowledged the power of God (see Daniel 6:21–22).

The Lion of the tribe of Judah is the only one who is worthy to break the seals and open the scroll before the throne of God. In Revelation 5:1-5 we read:

I saw in the right hand of Him who was seated on the throne a scroll written on the inside and on the back, closed and sealed with seven seals. And I saw a strong angel announcing with a loud voice, "Who is worthy [having the authority and virtue] to open the scroll and to break its seals?" And no one in heaven or on earth or under the earth [in Hades, the realm of the dead] was able to open the scroll or look into it. And I began to weep greatly because no one was found worthy to open the scroll or look into it. Then one of the [twenty-four] elders said to me, "Stop weeping! Look closely, the Lion of the tribe of Judah, the Root of David, has overcome and conquered! He can open the scroll and [break] its seven seals.

He alone is worthy to do what no one else can: take the scroll—which sets out God's comprehensive plan of redemption and restoration—break open its seals, and publish its glad tidings of great joy. Heaven's response is immediate: weeping turns into worship!

And there between the throne (with the four living creatures) and among the elders I saw a Lamb (Christ) standing, [bearing scars and wounds] as though it had been slain, with seven horns (complete power) and with seven eyes (complete knowledge), which are the seven Spirits of God who have been sent [on duty] into all the earth. And He came and took the scroll from the right hand of Him who sat on the throne. And when He had taken the scroll, the four living creatures and the twenty-four elders fell down before the Lamb (Christ), each one holding a harp and golden bowls full of fragrant incense, which are the prayers of the saints (God's people). And they sang a new song [of glorious redemption], saying, "Worthy and deserving are You to take the scroll and to break its seals; for You were slain (sacrificed), and with Your blood You purchased people for God from every tribe and language and people and nation. You have made them to be a kingdom [of royal subjects] and priests to our God; and they will reign on the earth." (Revelation 5:6-10).

KINGS

Many Christians are unaware of the fact that we are called kings and priests. *"You have made them kings and priests to our God; and they shall reign on the earth."* A king is a leader of people and oversees the principles and safety of the kingdom. A priest is the servant of the people and takes responsibility for the spiritual well-being of the people. In Christ, we are kings and priests, and we are to reign in life under the authority of the Reigning King Jesus. 1 Peter 2:9 says that we are a royal priesthood, and revelation confirms that Christ has "made us kings and priests unto God." Only Jesus is worthy of our worship:

Then I looked, and I heard the voice of many angels around the throne and [the voice] of the living creatures and the elders; and they numbered myriads of myriads, and thousands of thousands (innumerable), saying in a loud voice, 'Worthy and deserving is the Lamb that was sacrificed to receive power and riches and wisdom and might and honour and glory and blessing.' And I heard every created thing that is in heaven or on earth or under the earth [in Hades, the realm of the dead] or on the sea, and everything that is in them, saying [together], 'To Him who sits on the throne, and to the Lamb (Christ), be blessing and honour and glory and dominion forever and ever.' And the four living creatures kept saying, 'Amen.' And the elders fell down and worshiped [Him who lives forever and ever]. (Revelation 5:11-14).

He is the very King and Lord of our souls. When we say, "Lord, You reign," we are praying that King Jesus will reign within our hearts. We want to bow our hearts to His exalted name and confess that Jesus in indeed Lord of our lives.

Therefore God exalted him to the highest place and gave him the name that is above every name, that at the name of Jesus every knee should bow, in heaven and on earth and under the earth, and every tongue acknowledge that Jesus Christ is Lord, to the glory of God the Father. (Philippians 2:9-11).

The coronation of King Charles III means He is officially the royal head of state. The coronation of King Jesus means He is the head of the church—the body of Christ. How bright and glorious His kingdom is over other kingdoms. His reign is established over all creation.

The Apostle John says in the book of Revelation 14:14:

And I looked, and behold a white cloud, and upon the cloud one sat like unto the Son of man, having on his head a golden crown, and in his hand a sharp sickle. (KJV).

There is a kind of excitement that overwhelms us whenever we hear or know that a loved one is visiting soon. Our mind will just be going over all the things we anticipate will happen when the person arrives.

'Behold' means to see, observe, view, or watch something or someone remarkable and impressive. In the Bible, the word "behold" in both Hebrew and Greek denotes "look" or "see." 'Behold' is one of those wonderful English words that urges the mind to focus, think, pay attention, and understand.

We see that when Christ returns to this earth, He will have been crowned in heaven. The Bible speaks of the marriage supper of the Lamb, which will be like a royal wedding where the church, as the bride of Christ, will join the coronation of Jesus Christ.

What a sight that will be! All of us who have acknowledged Him as King here will be there in that day. My reservation is made. My seat is being saved at the marriage supper of the Lamb. My ticket is in my heart. It is the ticket to the greatest banquet of all time, paid for by the blood of Christ

141

upon the cross. The only thing that it cost me was my sins. I gladly renounce them and pay allegiance to the King of Kings before Whom I someday shall stand to give an account of my stewardship on earth. —Billy Graham

CHAPTER TWELVE
LOOK UP!

"They will [be privileged to] see His face, and His name will be on their foreheads. And there will no longer be night; they have no need for lamplight or sunlight because the Lord God will illumine them; and they will reign [as kings] forever and ever." (Revelation 22:4-5).

I recently watched a fireworks display at night, and as I looked up at the skies, I was in awe of the sound, the sparks, and the lighting released into the atmosphere. Then, I gazed far above the fireworks and saw the moon and stars. I watched intently, beholding the wonder of the God of creation who displays the moon and stars in the heavens above the skies. Then I recalled King David's expression in Psalms 19:1-5:

The heavens declare the glory of God; the skies proclaim the work of his hands. Day after day they pour forth speech; night after night they reveal knowledge. They have no speech, they use no words; no sound is heard from them. Yet their voice goes out into all the earth, their words to the ends of the world. In the heavens God has pitched a tent for the sun. It is like a bridegroom coming out of his chamber, like a champion rejoicing to run his course.

David is telling us that the heavens (the earth, moon, stars, and planets) declare the glory of God, and the skies proclaim the work of His hands. He goes on to say that despite having no speech, words, or sound, the days speak, and the nights reveal knowledge. Meditating on these verses in Psalms 19, some people may ponder these questions: Are there really things in the heavens that declare God's glory? Do the skies proclaim the work of His hands? Do the days speak? Do the nights reveal knowledge? Is there evidence that the moon and stars are set in place?

O Lord, our Lord, How majestic and glorious and excellent is Your name in all the earth! You have displayed Your splendour above the heavens. Out of the mouths of infants and nursing babes You have established strength. Because of Your adversaries, That You might silence the enemy and make the revengeful cease. When I see and consider Your heavens, the work of Your fingers, The moon and the stars, which You have established, What is man that You are mindful of him, And the son of [earthborn] man that You care for him? Yet You have made him a little lower than God, And You have crowned him with glory and honour. (Psalm 8:1-5).

Watching the fireworks display was more than an eye-opening event. As I looked around me, there were people of

144

all nations; families with children of all ages standing close to each other and celebrating the festive display with shouts of joy. My mind was getting a better understanding of what that moment will be like when Jesus comes on the clouds of heaven. Often, we take the sacred scriptures for granted. If we "look up" with more than just our natural eyes, we will see that there are lessons to be learned, important factors to comprehend and, sometimes, much discovery to be made. Whenever Jesus says, "He who has ears to hear, let him hear," He is calling for people to pay careful attention. It is another way of saying, "Look up! Listen carefully and pay close attention!" The readers of Revelation are called upon to pay close attention and seek God's insight and perspectives on specific details and the explanation of future events being revealed.

THE FATHER'S INSCRIPTION

The inscription above Jesus on the cross was so much more than just an inscription. The Latin title "Rex" has the meaning of "king, ruler, monarch." In Latin, the text "JESUS OF NAZARETH, THE KING OF THE JEWS" would have been written, "Iesus Nazarenus Rex Iudaeorum." The letters "INRI" were truly on the sign that Pilate placed over Jesus' head. John 19:20 says:

"And many of the Jews read this inscription, for the place where Jesus was crucified was near the city; and it was written in Hebrew, in Latin, and in Greek."

145

The sign was written in three different languages. This is widely known as a royal cypher, which consists of the initials of the monarch's name and title. The monogram is formally designed and affixed on a crown.

In the United Kingdom, the Royal cypher of the reigning sovereign was previously ER or EIIR for Queen Elizabeth II, and it will now be CR or CIIIR, meaning King Charles III. The letter "R" signifies "Rex" and has the meaning of "king, ruler, monarch," which is the same meaning as the inscription written on the sign above the head of Jesus on the cross.

As true servants of the Kingdom of God, we have the Father's name written on our foreheads. Many people may use a title with their names, like professor, doctor, honourable, Sir, Lord, President, Governor, Senator, King, Queen or Prince, but the children of God bear the Father's name.

Then I looked, and there before me was the Lamb, standing on Mount Zion, and with him 144,000 who had his name and his Father's name written on their foreheads. (Revelation 14:1).

The idea of having the father's name on the forehead and being sealed originated from the ancient practice of branding a slave with the name or mark of his master. So, the expression: *"His servants will bear His name upon their foreheads,"* shows absolute ownership. The forehead represents the one whose mind we have been given, which is that of Christ. In Philippians 2:5, we are admonished to have the mind of Christ: *"Let this mind be in you, which was also in Christ Jesus." (KJV)*. To have the name of God upon the forehead bears the truth of His people seeing everything through God's eyes. It is like seeing your reflection in a mirror. The Apostle Paul wrote:

For now [in this time of imperfection] we see in a mirror dimly [a blurred reflection, a riddle, an enigma], but then [when the time of perfection comes we will see reality] face to face. Now I know in part [just in fragments], but then I will know fully, just as I have been fully known [by God]. (1 Corinthians 13:12).

The Word of God is like a mirror reflecting God's knowledge and truth through His love, kindness, mercy, compassion, grace, forgiveness, and righteousness. The forehead represents the uppermost thought of the mind and conscious awareness of God as our heavenly Father. In the final chapter of the Bible, Revelation 22, it mentions that it will be the greatest privilege to see His face:

They will [be privileged to] see His face, and His name will be on their foreheads. And there will no longer be night; they have no need for lamplight or sunlight because the Lord God will illumine them; and they will reign [as kings] forever and ever. (Revelation 22:4-5).

This scripture gives us a vivid appearance of God's presence, His power, and His glory—the kind of power that resurrects, delivers, overcomes, and transforms. It is greater and stronger than any other power in existence. The majestic splendour of the Reigning King is evident from the appearance of His face, which beamed like the sun at its brightest time in the noonday. In fact, the light of His glory is so brilliant that no one can approach it.

KING OF GLORY

The phrase "King of glory" is ascribed to the Lord of hosts as found in Psalm 24. We see King David declare: *"He is the King of glory [who rules over all creation with His heavenly armies]. Lift up your heads, you gates; be lifted up, you ancient doors, that the King of glory may come in. Who is this King of glory? The Lord strong and mighty, the Lord mighty in battle. Lift up your heads, you gates; lift them up, you ancient doors, that the King of glory may come in. Who is he, this King of glory? The Lord Almighty—he is the King of glory. (Psalm 24:7–10).* "King of Glory" means that glory starts and ends with God—Alpha and Omega, Beginning and the End, First and the Last. The Bible tells us to fix our eyes on Jesus, the Author and Finisher of our faith. The coming of the King of glory calls for a time of celebration. He is the most strong and mighty King.

Let us worship the King of glory who is strong and mighty in battle. Kingdom believers can experience the glory of God when we pray that God's Kingdom come on earth as it is in heaven. Then, miracles, signs, and wonders will occur in the church and in our own personal lives. When believers gathered in a spirit of unity, seeking the Lord, the glory appeared in the upper room on the day of Pentecost, and sat

148

on the head of each person there (see Acts 2:1-4). Each born-again believer can manifest God's glory here on earth, but we must believe when we pray. Pray that you will understand the riches of the glory of His inheritance in the saints. When we inherited Him, glory was deposited in us, but we must allow the Reigning King to take full control of our lives—that is the revelation of what it means to experience the King of glory.

The disciples were more focused on the signs of the end times, but then Jesus told His disciples:

"There will be signs in the sun, moon and stars. On the earth, nations will be in anguish and perplexity at the roaring and tossing of the sea. People will faint from terror, apprehensive of what is coming on the world, for the heavenly bodies will be shaken. At that time, they will see the Son of Man coming in a cloud with power and great glory. When these things begin to take place, stand up and lift up your heads, because your redemption is drawing near." He told them this parable: "Look at the fig tree and all the trees. When they sprout leaves, you can see for yourselves and know that summer is near. Even so, when you see these things happening, you know that the kingdom of God is near." (Luke 21:25-31).

The return of Jesus on clouds with power and glory bears witness to the truth that He is the Reigning King. All power and authority is given to Jesus in heaven and over all the kingdoms of the earth. Rightly so, He will return from His resurrected home to show Himself again to the whole world as the Reigning King.

The book of Revelation is the unveiling of God's plan for the last days. It is the salvation package purchased through Jesus dying on the cross to destroy Satan, to deliver His people from sin, and to establish His kingdom of righteousness and peace on earth. All these great happenings will culminate in one great event to fulfil the Word of God in human history: the second coming of Jesus Christ. Jesus said, "Look, I am coming soon!" Revelation 22:12 says:

Behold, I (Jesus) am coming quickly, and My reward is with Me, to give to each one according to the merit of his deeds (earthly works, faithfulness). I am the Alpha and the Omega, the First and the Last, the Beginning and the End [the Eternal One].

Behold! Look Up! Rest assured, there is something worth looking forward to. A voice from heaven is pleading for our attention, saying "Come, stop, think, fix your eyes on Jesus. Look up! Look Up!" Are you looking forward to the great day of the Lord's appearing? When Jesus ascended, the wondering eyes of men looked on as He went through the clouds to be seated at the right hand of the Father's throne in heaven.

And after He said these things, He was caught up as they looked on, and a cloud took Him up out of their sight. While they were looking intently into the sky as He was going, two men in white clothing suddenly stood beside them, who said,

"Men of Galilee, why do you stand looking into the sky? This [same] Jesus, who has been taken up from you into heaven, will return in just the same way as you have watched Him go into heaven." (Acts 1:9-11).

The hour draws near when the Reigning King will appear from the clouds, and every eye shall see Him. Only a few men saw His ascension into heaven, but all men will see His return. The heavens will open, and the world will behold Jesus Christ in the fulness of His glory.

And I saw heaven opened, and behold, a white horse, and He who was riding it is called Faithful and True (trustworthy, loyal, incorruptible, steady), and in righteousness He judges and wages war [on the rebellious nations]. His eyes are a flame of fire, and on His head are many royal crowns; and He has a name inscribed [on Him] which no one knows or understands except Himself. He is dressed in a robe dipped in blood, and His name is called The Word of God. And the armies of heaven, dressed in fine linen, [dazzling] white and clean, followed Him on white horses. From His mouth comes a sharp sword (His word) with which He may strike down the nations, and He will rule them with a rod of iron; and He will tread the wine press of the fierce wrath of God, the Almighty [in judgment of the rebellious world]. And on His robe and on His thigh He has a name inscribed, "KING OF KINGS, AND LORD OF LORDS." (Revelation 19:11-16).

The white horse that Jesus rides on shows His victory and power to overcome all evil with His authority. Jesus and His holy angels will emerge victorious from the battle. Hallelujah! Imagine Jesus the Reigning King with the fiery eyes, the eternal royal crown, the robe dipped in His shed blood, and the armies of heaven dressed in clean white linen dazzling with divine glory in a heavenly procession. All this splendour is ordained by God, the Father, to honour Jesus, His only Son.

Jesus is indeed "Faithful and True." The "Word of God" highlights Jesus' role in creating the universe by speaking everything into existence; He is the living Word who became flesh to save us. "King of kings and Lord of lords" expresses Jesus' ultimate authority over all earthly kings and their kingdoms.

FINAL THOUGHTS

As I consider the recent controversies within the Royal Family, I remember the story of the prodigal son who was reconciled with His Father even though the other brother didn't quite understand it at all. Also, Joseph who was reconciled with his father and brothers. God reconciled the family and allowed forgiveness, mercy, love, and abundant provision. Another good example is that of Jacob and Esau. That is why God is the referred to as the "God of Jacob," because He restores broken hearts and bring peace to troubled families no matter how long it takes or how bad things appear.

God sent Jesus, His only Son, to die on the cross to reconcile the whole world of sinners to Him as our heavenly Father.

Jesus satisfied God's requirements for reconciliation, but each person must receive the terms of reconciliation: *"If you declare with your mouth, 'Jesus is Lord,' and believe in your heart that God raised him from the dead, you will be saved." (Romans 10:9).* Be assured that the Reigning King will bring hope and reconciliation to Prince Harry and his brother, Prince William, their Father, King Charles III, and the rest of the family. The zeal of the King of kings, the Lord of lords and the Prince of Peace will accomplish this.

We are called to be Christ's ambassadors. An ambassador is a personal representative sent from the head of a state. Just as a head of state sends an ambassador on a diplomatic mission, Christ sends us on a mission to represent Him in both words and actions. As Christ's ambassadors, we convey Christ's message of good news, and we live in ways that show God's love for the people we encounter everywhere we go. God has commissioned each of us as diplomats to share with others His message of love and peace. As kingdom keyworkers, we have been given the ministry of reconciliation, confirming that God is making an appeal through us.

THE MINISTRY OF RECONCILIATION

Read and declare this scripture for the royal family:

"For the love of Christ controls and compels us, because we have concluded this, that One died for all, therefore all died; and He died for all, so that all those who live would no longer live for themselves, but for Him who died and was

raised for their sake. So from now on we regard no one from a human point of view [according to worldly standards and values]. Though we have known Christ from a human point of view, now we no longer know Him in this way. Therefore, if anyone is in Christ [that is, grafted in, joined to Him by faith in Him as Savior], he is a new creature [reborn and renewed by the Holy Spirit]; the old things [the previous moral and spiritual condition] have passed away. Behold, new things have come [because spiritual awakening brings a new life]. But all these things are from God, who reconciled us to Himself through Christ [making us acceptable to Him] and gave us the ministry of reconciliation [so that by our example we might bring others to Him], that is, that God was in Christ reconciling the world to Himself, not counting people's sins against them [but canceling them]. And He has committed to us the message of reconciliation [that is, restoration to favor with God]. So we are ambassadors for Christ, as though God were making His appeal through us; we [as Christ's representatives] plead with you on behalf of Christ to be reconciled to God. He made Christ who knew no sin to [judicially] be sin on our behalf, so that in Him we would become the righteousness of God [that is, we would be made acceptable to Him and placed in a right relationship with Him by His gracious lovingkindness]." (2 Corinthians 5:14-21).

PRAYER OF RECONCILIATION FOR THE ROYAL FAMILY

Our Heavenly Father, we bless Your holy name. Let Your Kingdom come in the Royal Family here on earth as it is in heaven. Your throne works in perfect harmony to release power, hope, forgiveness and grace to every broken heart and troubled family. We speak healing, restoration, and truthfulness in every person in the Monarchy. We praise You, the Reigning King, for Your faithfulness from generation to generation. In Jesus' Name. Amen.

Now to the King of the ages [eternal], immortal, invisible, the only God, be honor and glory forever and ever. Amen. (1 Timothy 1:17).

Jesus rode a donkey; He will ride a white horse.

He came in humility and meekness; He will come in majesty and power.

He came to suffer for sinners; He will come to establish the Kingdom of God for His saints.

He came to seek and save the lost; He will come to judge and rule as King.

He came as the suffering Servant; He will come as King and Lord.

He was rejected by many as the Messiah; He will be proclaimed as the Reigning King forever.

Printed in Great Britain
by Amazon

17637353R00092